Praise for *Chef Interrupted*

'Trevis is not only a superb chef and a warrior in his quest to live with MS, he is also one of the most generous people I've had the fortune to call a friend. In the time I've known him, he's shared tales both funny and serious, sad and happy. He is a consummate storyteller, a magician with words. No matter his subject, he weaves a picture for you to imagine and invites you to join him in the world he's creating. I have no doubt that his story, as told in this engaging book, will touch readers profoundly, just the way he has touched my life.'

– Kathy Casey, Chef, Mixologist, author of *Sips & Apps*
(Chronicle Books, 2009)

'I had previously known Trevis Gleason only as the popular blogger at Life With Multiple Sclerosis. Within the constraints of this platform, he dispenses his wisdom, humour and charm in 500-word snippets. But in *Chef Interrupted* Trevis throws off the shackles of forced brevity and reveals his considerable storytelling acumen … I devoured the book in no time at all. It's a delightful read for anyone who longs to find meaning by going back to their roots, in this case his ancestral homeland of Ireland … And yes, it's about living a full life despite a debilitating disease.'

– Mitch Sturgeon, Enjoying The Ride Blog

'When I want to know what's really "cooking" in the MS community, I log onto Trevis' blog. He has never failed to provide balanced, candid, thoughtful, and even humorous insights into life with MS. His perspectives about the issues of the day – MS related and otherwise – always enlighten and inform me. The same is true for *Chef Interrupted*.'

– Joyce Nelson, CEO emeritus, National Multiple Sclerosis Society

'Don't think of this book as a how-to-cope tome. Trevis Gleason's *Chef Interrupted* has widespread appeal and is a joy to read. Certainly his prose abounds in Celtic wit and American audacity – plus a perfectly cooked attitude of use to people who have never heard (lucky them) of "multiple sclerosis". His recipe is not to devote his life to endless warfare against a nasty incurable disease or to collapse in saintly victimhood. He's just going on with it directly, indirectly, whatever direction works. I suppose the Irish have known this forever.'

— Martha King, Editor, *Momentum*, the magazine of the
National MS Society (USA)

'What I love about Trevis' writing is that he makes connections: with his blog followers, with people who have multiple sclerosis or live with other long-term conditions, with foodies, with just about anyone who reads what he writes. *Chef Interrupted*, like all of Trevis' writings, is instantly relatable, funny, smart, skeptical, hopeful, and always interesting.'

— Rose Pike, Executive Managing Editor, EverydayHealth.com

'Trevis is one of those truly gifted community organisers. To be able to lead and organise a community you have to have the ability to inspire. Trevis has this down to an art. I've seen him transform his pain into humour, humility, and personal growth via his writings, but perhaps even more impressive is his natural ability to relate to and reach people. That means he has the gift to make you give a damn to the point you find yourself repeating his musings to others. That's the mark of a talented writer and community leader.'

— Natalie Brown, Editor, *Health Talk*

CHEF
Interrupted

TREVIS L. GLEASON runs the award-winning Life With MS, a widely read and respected blog. An active contributor to EveryDayHealth. com, MSUK and the National MS Society (US), he is also on the editorial board of MS Ireland. He was twice ranked as No. 1 Online Influence on the topic of MS. He regularly gives talks and readings, and is on the organising committee of Dingle Food Festival. With his wife Caryn and their two dogs, he splits his time between Seattle and Kerry.

Stay up to date with Trevis at:

 www.trevislgleason.com

 www.facebook.com/LifeWithMS

 @TrevisGleason

To Herself, Herself and Herself –

The one who first brought my heart to Ireland
The one who stole my heart in Ireland
And the one who was waiting for my heart and
    brought it back to Ireland

Dingle, 2019

CHEF
Interrupted

DISCOVERING LIFE'S SECOND COURSE IN IRELAND
WITH MULTIPLE SCLEROSIS

To Vishauna

Happy Birthday

TREVIS GLEASON

The Collins Press

First published in Ireland in 2017 by
The Collins Press
West Link Park
Doughcloyne
Wilton
Cork
T12 N5EF
Ireland

First published in 2015 by Coffeetown Press, Seattle

Photographs © author's collection except for p. 16 (© Marilyn
Batali) and p. 218 (© California Culinary Academy).

Trevis L. Gleason has asserted his moral right to be identified as the author of
this work in accordance with the Irish Copyright and Related Rights Act 2000.

A CIP record for this book is available from the British Library.

Paperback ISBN: 978-1-84889-302-3
PDF eBook ISBN: 978-1-84889-611-6
EPUB eBook ISBN: 978-1-84889-612-3
Kindle ISBN: 978-1-84889-613-0

Typesetting by Carrigboy Typesetting Services
Typeset in MinionPro
Printed in Poland by HussarBooks

Cover photo by Manuella Agner

Contents

Contents

Part IV – December

Part V – The Journey Continues: Supper Recipes

Part VI – January

Part VII – The Journey Ends: Sweet Recipes

Introduction

LIVING WITH MULTIPLE SCLEROSIS (MS) has made me live my life in fast forward, but first there was an adjustment period. The events I'm about to recount transpired nearly five years after my diagnosis – five years during which more 'adjustment' was required than I prefer to recall. In that time, the career with which I'd identified myself was ripped away, a strong marriage crumbled, and a subsequent relationship faltered as I stumbled through the ruins of my former life.

I came to realise that MS is not a death sentence; it's a life sentence, and while anyone could step into the street and be hit by a bus, people living with MS have seen the bus. We've been hit by the bus and we know that for the rest of our lives we will walk along the bus route – with our backs to traffic.

With the help of the National Multiple Sclerosis Society, a crack-rehab psychologist and management skills gleaned from kitchen jobs around the country, I cleared away the rubble of my old life and found a new and hopeful path to tread, albeit a misty one. Through that mist, it is impossible to see one's future.

Multiple sclerosis doesn't steal away our futures; it steals what we thought and expected to await us in our futures. My bright flash of the obvious was that my 'retirement years' weren't going to find me seventy years old, in a canoe, fishing in some pond in Vermont. MS had already stolen much of my control of my left side, attacked my vision, and even – showing the true bastard of itself – taken away elements of my sense of taste on a number of occasions.

If I was to enjoy any of the things I'd hoped to be doing in my far advanced years after a career, I would have to start identifying what those dreams were and create a plan to make them happen.

Hope, without a plan, is just a dream.

The moment to which this whole, whacky dream of an idea can be traced is St Patrick's Day, 1977. Grade 5, West Elementary School …

On that day in a working-class suburb of a small Michigan city, my grade school teacher, one Mrs Ilene Magee, set in motion a series of events – both real and imagined – that led to a sleepless flight into a dark north Atlantic night. Belongings packed, apartment sublet, I would head out to pursue the next phase of my life, which would begin with a 180-year-old stone house, The Cottage, leased for the winter in the fabled fields of forty shades of green.

The first time I made the connection between my move 'home' to Ireland and Classroom #107 was as my former live-in girlfriend Beth and I drove from the railroad terminus in Sligo, in north-west Ireland, to my ancestral village in 'The North' on my first trip to the island. It was a most generous Christmas gift Beth had given me, that trip. Planes, trains, buses and taxis got us everywhere we wanted to be in counties Cork, Kerry, Dublin, Sligo and Fermanagh – to the wee village (wide spot in the laneway, really) whence my people came.

I was home again – for the first time.

I'd always held firmly to our family's Irish heritage, even in the absence of proof beyond family lore. The red hair of my youth, skin so white it shaded toward blue, save when it turned lobster-red at the hint of sun, freckles so prevalent they were something of an embarrassment, and my ability to put on an Irish accent whenever a laugh was called for were all the confirmation I needed that we were Irish.

Not until a few months before Beth and I began planning that first trip had anyone in the family bothered to do any real research into our family's Irish history. Only after flipping page after page after page (after page) of an incredibly detailed yet painfully vague Gleason Family History, assembled by my Aunt Sandy, a Gleason by marriage to my father's brother, did I find any reference to Ireland.

His name, this 'Irishman' with whom I'd fostered a life-long, anonymous relationship, was Josias, Josias Gamble. He was born on Islay, an island off the Argyll coast in Scotland ... SCOTLAND. He wasn't a Gleason and he wasn't even IRISH! Although, like many during the Plantations, he did marry Irish.

The Plantations were difficult for the Irish, as English overlords imported Scottish ruffians to act as foremen and overseers of their newly acquired land holdings, particularly in Ulster. Josias Gamble was one such scoundrel the British recruited to come to the island to work and generally harass the Irish villagers near Enniskillen. The great mistake in some cases – at least in the case of great-granda Gamble – was that some of this imported muscle had little more regard for the English than did the Irish.

Josias married an Irish girl in County Fermanagh and they had three sons. Some 330 odd years later I was born, his ninth great-grandson, in Grand Rapids, Michigan – a mutt, to be sure, but a mutt of Irish descent.

I knew of the name part. In the days of the Great Depression, formal adoptions by stepfathers were a detail and expense overlooked by far more than just my great-grandfather. It was to him that the County Tipperary name Gleason belonged: William Selah Gleason, born 1882. He married my great-grandmother, Marie (Andrews) Gamble and welcomed her son, my grandfather, Fred Darrel Gamble, into his home and, later, his business. This was possibly the most affirming form of acceptance for that generation of Americans. When he enlisted in the Army during the Second World War, my grandfather later – of his own accord – changed his name to Darrell Fredrick Gleason, after his stepfather.

Mine is the first generation in our family to have never met a Gamble. I was the oldest, and Darrell died two months and four days before I was born. That might be the reason I held tight to my Irishness when I was at school. Maybe it was a longing to connect to a family past, which to call 'murky' would be to call the journey in which I engaged over the winter of 2005/2006 a 'holiday'. Maybe I'll never know for sure why, but as I write this, I'm pretty much leaning back toward crediting Mrs Magee.

'Trevis!' the slight woman with a severe, frosted beehive, lording over her classroom in an orange chequered smock-dress, said of my wearing green-plaid jeans on that St Patrick's Day, 'If you ain't Dutch, you ain't much.'

Seriously? Who says that to a fifth grader?

There was only one other Irish boy in my class, Paul Slattery. He didn't draw the Western-Michigan-Christian-Reformed wrath of Mrs Magee, or if he did, I don't remember it. In fact, to be honest, not until the very moment of writing down this recollection did I put together her distaste for the green and her own married name 'Magee'. I'm only now guessing that it was her husband, rather than me, in whom lay her detestation.

Explains a lot, now that I think of it … The poor bastard!

Prologue

IN ORDER FOR YOU to understand this memoir as the 'after the fall' tale that it is, I suppose it is required that I explain just who I was before MS. Though traditionally known as a prologue, this next part, in my culinary mind, is more an *amuse-bouche* of my backstory.

Food has always been a means of exotic transport for me. Growing up at a white-bread time and in a homogenous place in America, the only international travel my family could afford was attending and eating at the rare ethnic festival or cultural celebration my town offered. Though I joined the US Coast Guard, studied navigation as my vocation, and began to travel the country, an interest in foods – and later cooking those foods – was my constant adult avocation.

When the time came to make a career change, I made wish lists of the fields in which I thought I had some talent – fields I enjoyed that could also make me a boatload of money. This was before the days of celebrity chefs, dedicated television networks and game-show culinary competitors, so the money part of my criteria wasn't likely to be in the cards were I to enrol at New England Culinary Institute in Montpelier, Vermont. Nevertheless, that's what I did in the autumn of 1990.

Even with an outstanding education and the reputation of a prestigious institution behind me, I felt a bit hamstrung by the fact that I'd never worked in a professional kitchen. Many of my fellow graduates had worked in their families' restaurants and hotels. In order to catch up with them and

Chef Trevis (*second from left*) with colleagues from around the world at an international culinary trade show in Los Angeles in 2000.

other new entries into the field, I worked numerous jobs at a time. A lunch cook by day, a tutor in the evenings and a catering cook on weekends, I began to work my way through the ranks of larger and larger kitchen brigades.

There is nothing more difficult or dangerous for a recovering egotist than to revisit periods and places from his past – and the person he (hopefully) once was. I would not be honest if I didn't admit that I networked nearly as much as I worked – and some former colleagues would say 'more'. My quick ascent was aided by talented mentors and fortuitous meetings; neither went unexploited. I hope the person you'll read about in the pages to follow is a much better man than I was 'before'. In short order, sous-chef positions became executive chef jobs. New England became New York and beyond. Consulting, writing, teaching and upper management jobs followed, and in ten short years after graduation, I was at the top of my game. I was good at my jobs, respected for my work, and I took full advantage of opportunities both offered and created.

My youthful travels through food eventually became travels because of food. I moved first to the former Soviet Union as part of an economic mission of the US government, then on to opening and running culinary schools throughout California, and finally to being appointed an executive chef with a German multinational, demonstrating equipment and training other (often world-renowned) chefs.

If ever there was a poster child for the old Hollywood saying, 'don't believe your own press,' it was Chef Trevis. Just at the moment I thought I could actually reach the outer edge of my ballooned persona – The Chef – MS stuck a pin into it and I was left to fight my way out of the collapsed, deflated shell.

I will never give this damnable disease credit for teaching me anything. I will, however, say that I have been a good student of what has been there to learn. When my former professional aspirations were stripped away, I was left with only my passion. Passion for food had been how I travelled. Passion then became why I travelled. Now my passion travels with me, inside of me, even though multiple sclerosis has taken it (and so much else) away as my professional pursuit. It is appropriate, therefore, that you will find culinary references throughout the pages to follow. It is also why I share a few recipes as well. Passion.

Chef Trevis serving guests at his own birthday party with chef Armandino Batali, in Seattle, 2006.

PART I

Before

1

The Town

THERE ARE MOMENTS IN our lives that change everything
– *everything.*

Some of these moments we understand as they occur.
One key moment of life-changing significance was lying,
for instance, on a cold X-ray table, balanced over a foam
triangle like an inchworm caught mid-rectilinear step,
awaiting the radiologist's 3½ inch, 25-gauge needle to 'slip'
between my fourth and fifth lumbar vertebrae and drain
three vials of my cerebrospinal fluid. I would have been
daft not to recognise it as such.

How could I have known, however, that such a moment
was underway as well when years later my younger brother,
Billy, and I stood together, arms around each other's
shoulders, equally in physical support as in camaraderie?
Under a Bulmers Draught Cider sign, swinging in a cold
February wind at the drinking-up hour, we sang at the
top of our lungs to our sister Angie's darkened B&B room
window three floors above the street.

'Angie! Aaaaann-gie!' Mick and The Stones would have
been so proud.

Nine months to the day from our impromptu concert
I would be living there, in that very town, fulfilling a
childhood dream – a dream I'd all but given up.

To say, however, that this drunken night was the impetus for my move to the small town in the southwest of County Kerry in Ireland (hereafter only to be referred to as 'The Town') would be a half-truth. Akin to saying that the American Revolution actually *began* on Concord Green in 1775 or that the Irish Potato Famine, *An Gorta Mór* (or The Great Hunger), was due to one bad crop. The truth of the matter is that I had a closing window of opportunity, afforded me by hardcore doses of corticosteroids coupled with a regimen of chemotherapy.

I live with multiple sclerosis (MS), a degenerative disease of the central nervous system that can (and often does) affect most of the body's functions. The way MS is thought to work begins with members of the body's own defence system deciding that the protective coating of the nerves that lead from the brain, down the spinal cord and out to every part of the body would make a tasty little snack. The immune cells – both T-cells and B-cells, it is now thought – attack the myelin sheath, which is the protective, fatty coating of our brain's axons. These axons are the long extensions of neurons or nerve cells, and the rogue immune cells are even thought to munch on oligodendrocytes, which produce the myelin coating.

The way I've illustrated it for years is to think of the brain as a telephone receiver (this would be a landline phone) and every other part of the body as another phone. Looking at the telephone poles that line almost every street in the developed world, we see copper wires that connect one phone to another through a complex system of grids and routers and such – not unlike the central nervous system. On the outside of those wires is thick, black rubber insulation. This insulation is the target of my errant immune system.

Envision now that some of this insulation has been stripped from the wires, exposing the signal-transmitting copper. The assault on any particular part of that wiring – and subsequent inflammation at the site of this damage – is known in the MS world as an 'exacerbation', an 'attack'. During such attacks, the inflammation causes an onset of symptoms on the part of the body to which that 'wire' is connected. Now, think of the long-term effects on the copper wire of that telephone line being exposed to the elements. The wire will corrode and swell and its integrity will deteriorate and negatively affect its ability to carry a signal. Think of the quality of the conversations you might have over such a telephone line.

You might, on some days, hear the conversation just fine. On other days, it might be static or you might hear only every other word. Or your conversation might get crossed with another signal passed on by the damage. You might not be able to hear the other line at all – ever again. Legs, eyes, bladder, hands, feet, muscles, organs, motor function, sex, digestion … you name it. There is no part or function of our bodies that cannot be affected by the insidious thief that is multiple sclerosis. Every one of us who lives with the disease knows this.

✦ ✦ ✦

My journey with MS began on a Monday morning – 23 April 2001, to be exact – and it began in the dark. I was in rural western New York for the weekend and had a very early connecting flight from Buffalo, through Minneapolis/ St Paul, back to Seattle. I was tired that morning, very tired, but it wasn't anything that caused worry.

The previous ten days had been hectic, but not particularly busy relative to my normal schedule. I flew a lot for business back then. In that week and a half, I'd flown on business to San Luis Obispo in California, Hawaii (three different islands), Seattle, San Francisco, Portland, Chicago and then on to upstate New York. Busy but not atypically so; thus 'tired' might be a bit of an understatement. My plan had been to spend a night in my own bed on Monday and catch up on office work, then fly back to San Francisco on Tuesday night.

I didn't end up making that San Francisco trip.

The first sign that something was going wrong (and we never see those 'first signs' until we're looking back on them) was when the woman driving me to the airport said that I was 'acting loopy' on the ride. My speech was erratic and I would zone out, mid-sentence. I chalked it up to the aforementioned travel itinerary; it was an easily justified assumption, looking back at that schedule.

This was pre-9/11, so the stresses of travel were far fewer than they are today. Passing through security, I picked up my overused mobile phone and started making my litany of business calls. In one conversation, I remember remarking how the airport concourse was doing one of those 'horror film' things – you know, where the whole corridor expands in front of the doomed protagonist? In that conversation, I also recall saying that it was as if I were walking thigh-deep through a swimming pool – such was the difficulty of my slog to the gate. It's a symptom descriptor that I now know all too well.

'I have got to get some rest,' I said as I hung up from my last call.

Let it be known that, back in the day, flying over 250,000 miles a year had a few benefits. Not the least of these, and especially on this day, was the automatic upgrade to a first-class seat. I would normally have spent the next several hours and two flight legs clicking away on my laptop computer and scouring paperwork while enjoying pretty decent airline service. On this day, from the moment I buckled my seatbelt low and tight across my lap, I slept.

I did not hear the security announcements, I did not feel take-off, I did not enjoy a first-class meal, and I did not feel our landing. I slept. I was alone in my row of two wide, leather seats. Had the cabin not become boisterous during disembarkation, I might have taken off again from Minneapolis to wherever the crew was headed on the same plane. I felt as if I actually had to travel from Minneapolis to St Paul in order to catch my connection. I can still remember the pain and total exhaustion that overcame me as I trod my way step by increasingly difficult step from my arrival gate to the distant departure gate. It was fortunate that my old travel agent had booked a two-hour layover. I don't think I could have made my connection otherwise.

Second verse same as the first when it came to the flight to Seattle – dead-to-the-world sleep.

From the Seattle-Tacoma International Airport, I drove ninety-odd miles to my home in Bellingham as late afternoon became early evening. My trusty ol' Jaguar must have known the route well enough to get us home safely, because I have no recollection whatsoever of the journey. As the evening in my loft-condo progressed, I began to note that something was wrong … seriously wrong.

Making my way from my study – where I had been catching up on local news and sorting paperwork for the next day – to the bar to refresh my drink, I began to realise the severity of the situation.

I had discovered the wonderful invention of radiant heating and had it installed under hardwood floors in my loft to replace the hideous carpeting that had covered every inch of floor when I bought the place. On cold winter mornings (or cool spring evenings like this one) the comfort of warm, wooden floors under bare feet can't be overstated. On this trek, however, I heard (and that's *heard*, not felt) my left foot slapping the maple flooring with every step. Looking down, I realised that I was lifting my foot, and my whole leg, from the hip and that my left arm was starting to feel heavy as well.

'Good God, am I having a stroke? I'm only thirty-five!' I wondered aloud as I thought about reaching for the phone but chose, rather, to reach for the gin.

For several days of that tangled travel itinerary, I'd been experiencing a real humdinger of a knot in my left trapezius (a back muscle). This thing felt like it was the size of a baseball, and I chalked up my left-side issues to the sinewy snarl likely pinching a nerve or something. I'd done this with mild symptoms for a good number of years – neglect them until they would not be ignored and then make excuses and brush them off. The body of evidence that things were going sideways had been building since early morning, and I was beginning to feel that it could no longer be easily brushed aside.

By the time I was able to wrench myself half-awake out of bed, early morning had passed. The first look in the bathroom mirror brought my mind to full alert. The face that stared back at me was drooping on the left side and felt doughy. Everything on that side of my body was slow to respond and thick when it did. Sitting to pee rather than trying to balance myself standing, I fell back to sleep on the toilet. Once I was awake again, I continued to accuse that ball of stress in my back muscle of causing all the trouble and made an appointment for a massage. What a 'guy' thing to do …

My massage therapist was more than just your average rub-down artist. She had advanced degrees and training in massage for cardiac, stroke and even catatonic/coma patients. This woman knew her way around a knotted muscle and then some. After seeing my tottering entrance and the state of muscle tone in my left limbs, she agreed to give me a massage, but only if I would go to the doctor directly after the appointment. I'll admit that I was beginning to think seeing a doctor was inevitable. Hearing her make the appointment for me as I undressed added to the dark thoughts that were pushing at the door to my consciousness.

From this point on in my recollection, the story seems to compress in my memory. If there is a mental version of the leap to warp speed, I think I experienced it. You know how sci-fi space travellers are momentarily immobilised and stretched just before being slingshot into the next dimension? That's how this part of the story goes for me. The journey from here to the MRI took place as a high-speed blur and snippets of tiny, dancing images.

From my warm and affirming massage, I was transported into the waiting room of my primary care doc, a locally respected sports medicine specialist and not easy to see on short notice. In the exam room, I remember downplaying my symptoms. I was a little embarrassed and apologetic to be taking up the doctor's time with my complaint. He was having none of it and I was secretly relieved to kick this ball into someone else's court. The gravity with which he was handling the case was simultaneously disconcerting and comforting.

In hindsight, I think he knew he was looking at a case of MS from the moment he took my history – profound fatigue, muscle weakness, electrical shock down the spine (that I now know to be Lhermitte's sign), erectile dysfunction … If ever there was a case of someone brushing off symptoms of something serious, it was a thirty-five-year-old man blaming erectile dysfunction on 'being tired'!

I have a pretty noir sense of humour; it has always aided me in the toughest of times. This experience was no exception. When I found myself unable to perform the requested heel-to-toe canter across the room, I went into my best 'Monster' from *Young Frankenstein* walk. When asked to touch my nose, eyes closed, with my fingertips, I quipped, 'Honestly, officer, I've only had a couple …'

As if set into inevitable motion, the examination was conducted in textbook fashion. After the doctor finished, he called a colleague in for a second opinion. They both muttered 'MS?' and ordered an immediate magnetic resonance image of my brain and cervical spine, with gadolinium contrast.

Waiting in a cheap hospital gown for my first trip into the MRI tunnel of love, I was abandoned by my caprice macabre. I have since found myself able to actually sleep during my MRI scans. That day, however, I was acutely aware of every click, thump and baritone shimmy of the machine. What horrors was this modern-day iron maiden finding as she sliced my brain and C-spine into lateral and peripheral views? How long was this going to take? How long had I already been in there? Was I going to die?

What?! Where in the holy hell had that one come from? From somewhere deep in my most secret and private nook, that question bubbled to the top like a stinking bubble of sulphur from the primordial sludge.

The words 'You have MS' are a shock to hear. Living with the ever-changing, sometimes debilitating symptoms of MS is a shock as well. Everyone with multiple sclerosis goes to bed knowing that the morning may find us without an ability with which we fell to sleep. We get up as best we can, and we make our way in life as best we can, while we can.

That … *that* is why I took on the challenge of living my dream in a small Kerry town for the winter. I didn't know how much longer actually living that dream would be a possibility.

In the words of my father, 'If you don't, you won't.' So I did.

🐦 🐦 🐦

The Town, I noted, as I waited outside a phone box while Billy called his wife – because drunk dialling is something of a family strength for us – had well beyond everything I would need to live. Although the full-time population census registers at fewer than 2,000, The Town is a thriving centre of tourism, come the summer months.

With a greengrocer, fishmonger, butcher, three super-markets (at least the Irish country version of such things) and pubs enough to support tourists, locals and the owners of numerous holiday homes, the 'infrastructure' of The Town surely met – hell, it exceeded – my needs. Its proximity yet distance to two larger towns (to be known only as The Larger Town and The Other Larger Town) afforded additional services as well as distractions, should The Town's quaintness begin to wear on me.

Up and down all the streets and lanes, as our fellow pub-goers tucked themselves behind colourfully painted doors, I could see neat stone-and-plaster buildings. A shop here, a pub there, a cosy flat one level up, and rows of homes, attached wall to wall, dimly lit with feathers of smoke trickling skyward from chimney and stove pipes alike.

That's another thing about The Town, any town in Ireland, really – The Smell!

Ireland is so unlike America, where one place runs into the next as if to keep you from realising when you've left one sprawling suburb and entered another. Driving from place to place in Ireland, when you arrive in a city, town, village or parish, you know it. During the colder months, you smell the place just before you see it.

The smell was not familiar to my American nose at first. It's a smell you can almost taste, like drinking the strong, bitter tea that the Irish love whilst burning a pile of dry oak leaves on wet clay at the first frost. To me, though, it is a smell that reaches across the centuries – the smell of the old ways hanging on, the taste of earth in the air brought forth by fire.

To me, it is the smell of home.

In the larger places, the few cities or towns that are some distance from agrarian lands, the smell is likely to be of coal. One can imagine it being burned on grates in open fireplaces in Dickensian fashion. Truth be told, many (if not most) who burn solid fuel in Ireland use a cast-iron stove, which is far more efficient than the large, open hearths we may imagine when we think of Irish cottages.

In the country, however, it isn't typically coal that is burned – well, not fully formed coal at least. Turf is really nothing but young, unfinished coal. Sods of this black-brown earth cut from ancient bogs in the lowlands with special shovels – a '*sleán*' or 'slane,' a longish spade with a sharp wing jutting off one side – are laid out in the sun for a couple of weeks and turned or footed several times to dry. They're then stacked for use as fuel for heating and cooking. Commercial versions of mechanically dug and hydraulically pressed turf, briquettes, can be purchased at nearly every village hardware store or at filling stations alongside a country road.

Now and again, if you're lucky, you can find old feedbags overflowing with hand-dug sods from a local farmer's bog. This turf is cut and dried the old way by someone who believes that owning land means working the land, that being a responsibility to the earth and its maker. That it results in a few extra euro for 'down the pub,' to boot, should never be frowned upon.

The next morning, still quite hungover from a night that began with too much wine and ended with less than favourable results for poor Billy in the phone box, we came upon a filling station with sacks of such turf being unloaded from a manure-speckled trailer towed behind a tractor. The man doing the unloading looked as gnarled and weathered as his equipment but was justifiably proud of his sacks of hard, black turf. I made note of the place, not far from one of the county's most famous strands.

We prepared the car and ourselves for the trip over the lyrically fabled Cork and Kerry Mountains and on into County Tipperary, the homeland of our adopted name. If I lived in The Town – and the plan was already beginning to form – I would buy this man's turf.

   🖋 🖋 🖋

I have an idiom of sorts when it comes to living up to my word: 'If I say it out loud …' as if verbalising a contract with the universe or anyone who might be listening. I fall short of my aspirations from time to time, but if I say my intention out loud, I'm going to give it one hell of a go.

Well, I said it out loud.

Not a week later, after I had dispatched my siblings, along with their weeping livers, into the care of Aer Lingus, I said it out loud to the woman who was to be my travelling companion for the second leg of this two-week trip.

'I'm going to take some time and live in Kerry, while I still can,' I told her as we lingered over after-dinner whiskey in front of the fire at a fabled sixteenth-century castle in County Clare.

I think I surprised myself a bit with my statement. I know it surprised my companion. We'd been involved in a tepid, in-between relationship. My announcement that I was leaving the country to play this travel card before MS took it out of my deck was the beginning of the end of that relationship – though it would linger, unattended to, like the wild fuchsia in hedgerows of Kerry, a while longer.

   🖋 🖋 🖋

The nine months back in Seattle – between singing The Stones with Billy and my intended flight 'back home' to Ireland – were occupied by more planning for my future than I'd done in the entire five years since my diagnosis.

Owing to my sometimes-impaired cognitive abilities, crushing fatigue and physical limitations, I was no longer able to work full-time. For the first couple of years after my diagnosis it seemed like the most I could do was just try to manage my care. Doctor appointments, insurance issues, paperwork – the likes I hadn't seen since establishing an international financing scheme for a co-op of farmer/bakers in Ukraine in the 1990s – all took far more time and painful amounts of energy than anything I'd ever experienced.

I had once been able to manage multiple foodservice outlets in a five-star hotel while developing curriculum and teaching classes at the adjoining university, write for a national newspaper syndicate and start a consulting business, while simultaneously maintaining a marriage and busy social life. Less than four years after my diagnosis and I could hardly recognise the person I'd become.

Double shifts, split shifts and the occasional eighteen-hour day are required in the food business. Sometimes, the simple act of getting myself from bed to bathroom for a morning pee exhausts my day's energy supply and six more hours of anaesthesia-like sleep ensue. When I had been sales director for a German multinational's US division, multi-unit deals, tiered discount structures, commissions, bonuses and back-end rebates rolled off my tongue in soliloquy without effort. Now, 'black holes' in my brain sometimes make numbers unrecognisable.

Most difficult to see drip away from me was my sense of passion. In love and in life, in vocation and in avocation, I had always been a full-tilt participant. MS robbed me of a career I loved, the financial stability that profession afforded, the energy to sustain my lifestyle and, through difficult bouts of depression, it sapped my passions.

In many ways, Beth's gift of taking me to Ireland had fanned what seemed like a final ember of passion within me – a spark I'd forgotten about or at least left unattended for a very long time. Though it took a great effort to complete even the simplest tasks, I felt an embryonic warmth growing in me as I found a house to let, made flight arrangements, and attended to the countless details the trip would require.

The last days leading up to any holiday are hectic. It oft feels that when we've finally finished preparing for the time away, we need it more than ever. How many times have we worked so hard to get caught up and work ahead for a two-week holiday that we spend our respite with a stress-related cold or some such? This trip was no different, save that I was to be away for a full three months!

PART II

November

2

Redeye

THE MORNING PRIOR to departing Seattle found me packing up the last few things I would be taking along.

I couldn't afford rent in both Seattle and Ireland, so I'd sublet my place to a Swiss researcher and his wife moving to Seattle for his job. They were looking for a base from which to search for a place of their own. I was looking for a way to cover my expenses while away and have the place looked after. I'd negotiated a very reasonable off-season rate for my lodging in The Town, so I wasn't going to be living like a tourist on holidays: I was going to be *living* in Ireland.

I would shortly be handing over the keys to The Swiss. My plans were well on their way to fruition, and I was about to see everything tied up in a tidy bow. Just one more day in Seattle followed by two days with my goddaughter's family near Boston before my quick overnight hop to my new 'home' in Ireland.

Imagine my surprise, hauling a rather large bag out the front walkway to the kerb and using a forearm crutch to aid the load, at finding an empty parking space where I had left my car. I must have looked a sight: mouth agape, head slapping back and forth as I gazed first up then down and back up my quiet residential street. For more than a moment I suspected a masterful stroke of practical foolery executed by friends. The few bits of broken window glass that flecked the pavement, however, were proof of a different kind of foolery.

My car had been stolen.

Rather than call the police then and there, as The Swiss were due any moment – and who would think an American police car in front of your new residence is a good first impression? – I thought it necessary to 'get Irish'. In other words, as had been my wont ever since multiple sclerosis began nibbling at my abilities, I had to improvise and overcome – traits for which the inhabitants of the home of my forebears have been noted for as long as there have been people on the island.

I quickly arranged transport with a neighbour, dragged my heavy bags to their kerb and readied the place for The Swiss. I filed my police report later in the morning, far AWAY from the house.

As a person writing a book, I should be able to convey the feeling I was experiencing that morning. I can't, however, describe it other than to say that the loss of my car was almost freeing. Letting the stress of having my means of conveyance taken away on the eve of this odyssey slip away like water from a duck's back was like shedding a connection to my life. It was as if I had loosed my bonds to one world, thereby freeing me to enter another.

The first lesson learned from my life with MS was that the only things over which we truly have control are our reactions and responses. My reaction to not having my car for the last twenty-four hours in Seattle may seem cavalier to some, irresponsible to others. What else was I going to do: cry? I'd cried enough in the previous years. I chose to laugh.

Besides, it was insured and I wouldn't need it for a while.

✒ ✒ ✒

Before leaving for my east coast jumping-off point, I delivered my first major fundraising speech for the National Multiple Sclerosis Society. A thousand-odd were assembled for the $150 rubber chicken salad luncheon and to hear Maureen Manley, a former world-class cyclist, speak about living with our disease.

I've spoken to crowds both larger and more intimate than were gathered that midday. Never before, however, had I had to ask people for their money. Never before had I felt the burden of need from thousands of people in my community hanging on the results of my words and the delivery of the same. I'm not one to shy away from a spotlight – I'm a Leo, after all. For this time, however, I'll admit to some unease.

An afternoon of post-event glad-handing – and keeping close watch on the accounting figures – fleeted into early evening and I became quite aware that I was desperately ready for a pint … and a bite. I realised that I had avoided the lunch part of the luncheon due to my uncharacteristic nerves.

Satisfied and celebratory, I left the event and walked from the convention centre toward a local tap. Seattle became appropriately damp, not unlike what November usually brings to the Pacific Northwest. Not unlike what I was expecting from the winter weather in Kerry. After slipping on the wet pavement as I turned into Post Alley near the Pike Place Market, I picked myself up, brushed myself off and ducked into The White Horse Trading Company. White Horse is a favourite watering hole of the local intelligentsia and in-the-know hipsters. I was well up for a drink to celebrate the record-setting donations made at the luncheon and eager to eat dinner (by now I was famished) and contemplate my adventure yet to come.

It's not uncommon to recognise a few faces at The White Horse; it's that kind of place. What awaited me inside the door, however, was more than a few. A farewell gathering had been arranged as a surprise. I guess I'd been so caught up in my departure that I hadn't really thought about the goodbyes. My ability to multitask was once a trait I took pride in and upon which I heavily relied. MS took that away from me and it was good to know that friends would attend to the periphery when my focus narrowed.

One pint led to a session and plenty of good craic.

By the time we finished the night, we had migrated down the alley to Kells Irish Pub and more than a few empty glasses were left in our wake. Most of a bottle of 'Tully' (what my family calls Tullamore D.E.W. whiskey) was in us, our numbers were down to a scant few and evening had turned to night and night into early morning … without a single bite to eat.

Goodbye smiles became tears, and hugs morphed into wet, goodbye kisses. I made it to my friend's flat, where I was to spend my last night, to find that there was hardly any night left. I was completely hockeyed by the drink and the hands of the bedside clock were far nearer the morning alarm than they were to midnight.

My eyes closed to the flashing of a nearby lighthouse beacon against the blinds and opened to it again – the only light of the still-dark dawn.

Looking into the vanity mirror while brushing my teeth, I was reminded of the line my chief boatswain's mate had bellowed at me one morning on my first Coast Guard cutter. It was one of the several mornings we had all shown up to quarters dangling somewhere between the night's drunkenness and the morning's hangover.

'Jackie,' – my unrequested nickname on that ship, harking back to 'The Great One' (the American entertainer Jackie Gleason) – 'your eyes look like two dog piss holes in the snow.'

They felt like it too.

*   *   *

As if one drunken going-away party wasn't enough, my last two nights on the continent *were* enough.

Boston's North Shore had been home to my former wife, Sheri, and me for the first four years of our marriage while I served my last tour as a Coast Guard Navigator before moving to Vermont for culinary school. We have friends still living there, the likes of whom could never be replaced. In the forty-nine hours I lay over in their town, the whole lot of dear ones made sure that my eyes were once again bloodied and feeling not unlike those puppy piddle pricks in polar precipitation.

It was as if they all thought it their job to ensure that I was properly conditioned for the pubs of Kerry.

With no brightening in the sky to be seen out of the airplane windows, we broke our cruise and began the descent. I made a quick trip to the lav to wash my face and brush the marching band from my teeth. I was finishing up when the captain's Dublin accent announced our imminent arrival into Shannon International Airport: Ireland's Welcome Mat for Americans.

A look into the polished aluminium of the Airbus lavatory mirror and I couldn't help but grunt aloud.

'That's why they call 'em Redeye flights, I guess.'

I was going to have to stop looking in mirrors the mornings after the nights before. A hot mug of tea and a proper Irish breakfast were called for and I knew just the place.

3

Ireland's Welcome Mat

AIRPLANE LANDINGS IN Europe are not the raucous affairs they used to be.

The touchdown of my first flight abroad, to Hungary in 1997, nearly brought the aircraft's occupants to their feet in wild hysterics, the likes of which I'd only seen once before. This happened after an absolutely heroic landing on Kodiak Island, Alaska, at the conclusion of an approach during which I could make out prayers in at least three languages. Even the landing of my first flight to Ireland with Beth, just a few years before this trip, allowed our flight crew awareness of our appreciation upon landing in Ireland. Although, now that I think of it, it may have been the elation of the London stag night boys at being away from their wives and only a short dash away from the pubs at the root of all of that hooting and hollering. Funny how dignified 'Let's get pissed, lads!' can sound when shouted by a covey of English barristers.

Only a perfunctory round of applause patted the air upon this arrival.

There was a small scurry of activity as a group of teens wagered how far the packet of airline-brand peanuts they'd set a-sliding would make it down the aisle as the rest of us planted our noses into the seats directly ahead. I am usually able to tell whether a pilot was trained in the Air Force or the Navy by how much runway he/she did or did not use, Navy pilots being trained to land on the short decks of aircraft carriers and all. Judging by the two-footed application of brakes by Your Man from Dublin, he'd come up landing on small sandbars and dead-end streets.

As the rest of us checked our foreheads for rug burn, all but one of the teens let out a collective disappointed groan. The lad now pumping his fist and cursing in a midlands accent must have wagered the aforementioned snacks would go the farthest, for they had coursed past the coach seats, through First Class, and all the way to the feet of a cabin attendant at the forward bulkhead.

As money changed hands to the victor, who was still taunting the vanquished with what I can only assume was a cloud of blue assaults (I couldn't understand a single accented word by this point in the one-sided volley), we were informed of the local time: not even 5.45 a.m. yet.

I had chosen this flight to Shannon because of its scheduled 5.45 a.m. arrival. By the time your American passport breezes you through customs and immigration and the rest of your fellow bleary-eyed passengers are assembling around the still silent baggage carrousel, you can be the first in the queue when the currency exchange window opens for 6 a.m. and the scones are still hot in the upstairs canteen.

Early winter tailwinds or a yet-to-be-discovered thinning troposphere had pushed us across the Atlantic night in less time than it took Lindberg to pre-flight the *Spirit of St Louis*.

The tired yet distinguished-looking customs officer gave me only a short, Vatican-influenced glance over his reading glasses when I told him the intended duration of my stay. 'Eighty-nine days,' I said. This number was just one day shy of the three-month limit on the grant of a tourist visa. I was, of course, prepared with paragraphs of explanation for the length of my visit: 'doing it while I still can, Irish family history, stone cottage, Fermanagh family, Irish puppy …'

STAMP!

Done, save for a quick red pen circle around the 'ninety-day' bit on the visa as silent reminder that I was a guest in his country. He didn't say 'Welcome to Ireland. Thanks for the dollars, Yank. Now go home' … aloud.

*   *   *

When the charge nurse wakes you for your fourth vital sign check of the night and you're trying to remember if you have to pee and you've blocked the anguishing memory of catheter removal or if gravity is now taking care of nature's call, all you hear is the low humming of a floor polisher somewhere around the corner and the sound of people coughing themselves awake. The same goes for the Shannon International Airport at 5.30 a.m., except for the peeing part. I was pretty damned sure I had to go.

Did I not mention spastic bladder issues with my old friend MS? Arrrgh!

They may escort nearly 2 million people per year in and out of the country from this relatively small air hub. At this hour, however, that bag of airline nuts could make it from one end of the building to the other without a single person seeing it, let alone be occluded in its voyage by anything or anyone. No one would even be around to lay odds on its potential progress.

Accustomed to their privileged niche in the world, freshly immigration-accepted visitors from 'The States' lined up at the car hire desks and began to huff indignantly that they weren't being served. Never mind that the cardboard cut-out clock at each counter advises to return at 6 a.m.; we have Ireland to 'do', villages to invade and pubs to crawl.

The sun would not be up for another two hours? So what!

I, on the other hand, hobbled my way up the stairs to the IKEA-designed breakfast room, found a hard bench, apparently salvaged from a monastic confessional, and waited for the scones to make their way to the serving line and the world-revered, impenetrable barrier that is the neoprene band across two chromium stations to be removed so I could enter and breakfast.

Within moments of disembarking, I was made aware of the return of the on-again-off-again pain of neuropathy in my left foot. Neuropathy (sometimes called neuropathic pain) is a funny thing – and I'm talking funny 'peculiar' here, not funny 'ha-ha'. It's real pain, sometimes even debilitating pain, but its cause isn't at the site where the sensation is experienced.

Somewhere along the nerve pathway from where my left peroneal nerve finds my spinal cord and the somatosensory cortex of my brain, some of that 'corrosion' I described had occurred, and I have a lesion. The result of normal signals passing from my foot and leg through this damaged area and on to the pain centre of my brain was causing me to feel pain. While there was nothing wrong, as in an injury or burn to that area, the pain was very real. Very.

Neuropathic pain is sometimes described as a 'burning' or 'tingling' sensation. That may be the case for some but for me it's more like the acute sensation of striking the 'funny bone' in your elbow. It may be called the humerus, but I can assure you there is very little humour in it.

I typically use a technique I learned in a pain management study that retrains the brain's reaction to pain. Through Cognitive Behavioural Therapy (CBT) – the same treatment now used for some veterans with Post Traumatic Stress Disorder (PTSD) and some Traumatic Brain Injuries (TBI) – I am able to dissect the pain experience from the place of pain, all the way through what I call 'the pain onion', to the pain reaction.

The actual pain never goes away. By controlling the cascade of negative thoughts associated with the pain, I can usually live with the experience, which can last for hours or months.

Today, however, with a multi-hour drive in a geared car ahead of me and three liver-punishing days with little slumber behind, I chose the pharmaceutical route.

I decided that it wasn't a bad idea to pop at least part of one of my anti-fatigue pills. These little puppies are actually an anti-narcolepsy med and cost about as much as a semester's tuition, books, plus room and board at Cornell. Many medical insurance policies don't cover this drug for multiple sclerosis, as it is officially 'off label' for MS, mine included. Some MS patients even resort to sharing the med with friends whose insurance does cover the cost.

A quarter of a pill dose can usually get me through a particularly tough bout of MS fatigue, but at a cost higher than coin. The energy 'chequebook' of those of us with MS has a finite daily balance and the drug is like a loan shark.

To say that we 'get tired' does it no justice. We're talking about lie-down-or-fall-down tired here. The drugs can get me through a day, but I'm only borrowing energy from the next day's balance. Two or three days running is about the extent of the efficacy in my experience. After that, even the loan shark drug can't pay my energy debts, and I lose a week to what the medicos call 'profound fatigue'.

I decided on a full pill.

The last of my nine-dollar, 3½ ounce (100 ml), airport-purchased, zero-calorie, gluten-free bottled water was used for washing my fangs upon approach, so I'd have to swallow the 800mg horse pill dry. I began saving up spit as I dug through one bag then another to find my prescription bottle. By the time I found the drug and attempted to crack the soviet-designed adult-proof lid (they should use these things as locks on our new border protection system) I had half of Lough Erne – the lake of my ancestral county – in my gob.

As if on cue, a matronly employee of the canteen saw me, puff-cheeked and wrestling with Stalin's pillbox, and came to the border gate. Her warm and distinctive Irish accent (I'm pretty sure she's from Poland) startled me and I turned my head like a Pavlovian mastiff – my spittle now equally divided between my chin, my sweater, and the confessional bench.

'We're not open for a tick, but you can come in for tea … if you like.'

The 'if you like' was more 'iv ug lick' as her brogue foundered into her native accent when she realised the possible error in having invited a drooling lunatic in for tea.

4

Skate-Ball Bag

STUFFED LIKE A FOIE GRAS goose on a traditional Irish breakfast of eggs, rashers, sausages, potatoes, mushrooms, tomato, beans, toast, tea and a currant scone, I found that the drugs had begun to work and I no longer had to hobble to the car-hire desk. Rather, I waddled under the mass of my pre-dawn meal.

Your Man at the internationally recognised yellow rental-car counter noted that I had a reservation for eighty-nine days.

'You know, you can't have a car for three months,' he said.

I'd later note that he used a distinct 'th' sound in that number rather than the lyrical 't'ree,' which I'd been practising and can be heard in nearly all Hollywood films about the country.

Now I began to feel that indignant American huff beginning to swell within me, but I soon realised it was simply the overloaded contents of a bacon-assaulted belly.

While the finer intricacies of Irish car-hire laws were recited (and you really should pay attention to the part about insurances), I got the general idea. I had a reservation for *a* car for the next three months, not *one* vehicle. Four weeks is the maximum time any one car can be rented so

I'd have to return the one I picked up today and exchange it for another within that allotted time. While the four-hour drive simply to swap conveyance might seem onerous (and surely would be), I would be back to this post to pick up visitors twice before the month was up and several more times during my stay. In total, I'd only have eleven days without house guests, so it shouldn't be an issue.

'I'll still get the same rate?' I inquired, as I'd booked online, and considering that Christmas holidays were smack dab in the middle of this rental, I'd secured a hell of a low rate.

'Awk, sure. It'll be grand,' he assured me. It wasn't …

* * *

I am old enough to remember the days when cars in Europe were exotic versions of the land yachts that rolled off Detroit's assembly lines. The continental takes on the American models were sleek and sexy and … well, foreign. The first car I hired in Sligo with Beth, for instance, might have been a Ford Taurus, but it looked more like a baby Jaguar or a Lexus-lite.

Having never driven on the 'wrong side' of the road from the 'wrong side' of the car, Beth and I decided it would be best to experience the process first, so we hired taxis to take us to our Cork city B&B and around places we wanted to visit for the first part of our trip.

It is amazing how much you can learn from a taxi driver.

Not all of them, of course, are techniques you'd want to be using in your every drive-a-day world. The basics of turning, signalling and the negotiation of roundabouts, however, can be gleaned by paying close attention. If your senses are acutely tuned, you may even pick up a curse word or two in the local tongue; it's how I knew that the young man on the plane had been regaling his mates with language from the violet side of the spectrum.

As for those roundabouts – also known to me as a 'rotary', 'traffic circle' and 'vehicular vortex of doom' – they make SO much more sense in Ireland than in America. Here, you enter from the left, rotating clockwise, exiting in orderly fashion, and indicating. This smooth system of transition of direction is, for some reason, as yet unknown to my people. My very first experience with the unregulated convergence of throughways was on the Cape Cod side of the Bourne Bridge late on a Friday afternoon in July.

It was that experience whence my calling them 'vehicular vortex of doom' evolved, after prescription anti-anxiety drugs were washed down with a litre of vodka cranberry. It's no wonder they called that drink a Cape Codder; I needed to be fed three of them through a straw just to pry my alabaster fingers from the steering wheel after that hot mess. Upon inspection of my allotted transport this day, I was quite happy to know that I would be exchanging it – maybe within four days rather than stretching it out for the full four weeks.

This was not a trim-looking American makeover nor was it something I would have normally thought of as a 'car' at all. If a bowling ball satchel and roller skate had met in the back room of a 1970s-era Rolo-Bowl-o-Rama entertainment facility in Up-Too-Tight Ohio and done the nasty to the romantic song styling of Gloria Gaynor and the 7-10 splits, this car would have been their love child. Bulbous on top, with a straight and non-aerodynamic hatchback, the car had a wheelbase that looked as if I should (and could) take a skate key to widen and broaden in order to strap it onto a giant's shoe.

I'd owned skateboards with larger tyres as a pre-teen, and though the car was the current year's model, I can only assume its odometer had been tampered with, as it looked far more rugged even than its 647,393-kilometre reading would suggest – though that could have been a kilometre/ miles conversion thing. I'm just sayin' …

If living with an ever-changing disease teaches one lesson, it's that the only things over which you have any real control are your reactions.

My reaction was to take the keys from Your Man (a different Your Man than Your Man at the auto rental counter – and might I interject here my appreciation, as a person who is always forgetting people's names, for the local pronouns of Your Man and Your One? We don't have such familiar efficiencies of language in America) and load my two suitcases, carry-on and briefcase into this 'skate-ball bag'. After filling the boot, the back seat, the passenger side – including the floor – and the rear window with my luggage, I was left with just enough room to close the driver's side hatch (as long as I shed my coat and sweater, rolled them up and wedged them behind my knees).

5

Drive on the Left, Idiot! Drive on the Left

AS THE CAR SLUNG-SHOT around and out of a half a dozen roundabouts (quite possibly on two wheels at times), running on both cylinders, a beautiful day was dawning over the whole of the island.

Judging time to distance in Ireland is not something one should do without significant conditioning. It is only about 160 kilometres (100 miles) from one coast to the other as the crow flies at my current latitude and less than 200 kilometres (120 miles) to watch the sun rise over the Irish Sea. If you stay on the main roads, I'd say it would only take one (keeping farm machinery and the odd shepherd's flock in mind, of course) about six days to get there. That is IF you stay on the main roads, mind – and I'm sure the skate-ball bag could make the trip and halfway back again on one tank of fuel. I only had eighty-nine days, though, so I decided not to attempt the endeavour.

A few more intersections and I was finally past Limerick city. Another turn or two in the road and I was driving along the N – (oh, never-you-mind which) National Road and slipping into the picturesque Irish countryside.

To assist me in staying in line with the local driving custom, I have chosen a simple mantra. At every turn, bend, roundabout, busy intersection or long country straight stretch, I find it helpful to state aloud:

'Drive on the left, Idiot! Drive on the left.'

It's only failed me a couple of times in the past, and forty-five minutes into this drive, I'd gone the entire way without a single slip-up.

I avoided the new dual carriageways in favour of the older, often more direct, routes that connect villages and towns together along ancient footpaths and lanes. They're the kind of roads farmers used to get from farm to town, barn to field, field to field. Judging by the tractor-to-car ratio, they are still using them for the same purpose.

The sun now in its full, late autumn glory caused me to smile, and I couldn't help myself from laughing … giggling really, like a schoolboy twenty minutes before the final bell of the term. Many back in America's Pacific Northwest asked me, 'Why would you move to Ireland in the winter?!' My response was a steady, 'Why would you stay in Seattle in the winter?!' A photo of any slice of my current visual arc would have provided a far better answer.

The fields aren't as green in November as I've seen in the tourist brochures or coffee table books, and those are the only places I've seen them in their glossy, glorious greenness. Three trips I'd made to the island since my first and each one was between October and February. While that might seem odd to some, it makes perfect sense to me.

I learned, while living in Vermont and attending culinary school, that Robert Frost, perhaps the state's most famous resident, never wrote a single poem about the magnificent foliage that people travel from around the globe to experience. Rather, in his poem 'Reluctance,' I found one of his rare mentions of leaves. He described the beauty and introspection that can be found when the leaves have changed their beautiful colours and fallen atop crusted snow, leaving us amid the raw remains of nature to find our own joy in the world.

Winter in Kerry may not offer itself up as a playground for the casual tourist, but I was not approaching the season as a tourist. I was not yet forty years old and had come to the early understanding of the importance of living in the stark light of the present rather than in the fading images of our past or the misty, blue fog of the future. Living with MS has a way of scraping away the glossy bits of our plans and dreams, leaving us to examine what remains – the real joys in life, not the fluff. Ask any 'real' chef about their dream meal, for example. It's a game that my mentor chef Michel LeBorgne used to play with his students at New England Culinary Institute – 'My Perfect Meal'. Students were asked what they would eat, where they would eat it, with whom they would dine, what they would drink, and to what they would be listening.

Lobsters, foie gras, caviar and exotic fare top the students' lists, while, to a person, the instructors of the school (and I later learned in conversations with some of the greatest chefs in the world, almost every 'old school' culinarian) wistfully request 'the perfect roasted chicken'.

The fuchsia hedgerows may be without leaves or flowers, the fields may show as much brown and grey as green, the matted sheep on the windblown hills (and in the roads!) are as far from their slick-sheared, springtime selves as they can be, but it seems to be the right time to be here.

This isn't a season of tourists and luxury motor coaches crowding the Ring of Kerry, frolicking on the beaches or dining on lobsters stuffed with goose liver and salted fish eggs. It is the rugged season, a time for stout men and hearty women driving shit-spattered farm equipment, a time for stacking the turf and topping off the oil tank. It is the time of the year for coarse brown soda bread, buttermilk scones, shepherd's pie – and perfectly roasted chickens.

I hoped it was also the time for a poser like me who was trying to live the experience but couldn't afford a rental in the high season, bouncing around in a skate-ball bag.

'Drive on the left, Idiot! Drive on the left!'

6

Sheep in the Garden

THERE ARE TWO ROADS INTO The Town and three roads
out. One can enter via the coast road or the mountain road.
As for the leaving, you can take the third road but it will
only loop itself around for a good hour's drive and deposit
you back at the point you've departed.

I decided to make my Sunday morning entrance via
the mountain road, with the hope of spying my winter's
dwelling along the way. I'd only seen the place on the
Internet, but I thought I might have spotted it as I passed
the drive. I couldn't be sure, though, as the tick-tick-ticking
sound the roadside hedges made against the skate-ball
bag's passenger-side mirror changed to a 'CLUNK' when
my eyes left the road for too long. I'd lost a mirror and €50
that way before, so I turned back to eyes front.

Whether it was or was not The Cottage would soon be
resolved, I realised, as I rang the doorbell of my landlady's
bed and breakfast where email arrangements had been
made to pick up the key. The landlady, I would later find
out, was something of a princess in The Town – a princess
in a town that no longer saw the need for a king. Other than
our email exchanges, I had spoken with The Princess once
via telephone. Her voice was the perfect cross between that
of Meryl Streep and surprised swan. She pronounced my

The Mountain Pass Cottage.

name more like 'Traeviuz' than Trevis, which is a far cry prettier than I've heard it pronounced in my native County Fermanagh. There, two syllables became one, and my mashed-together name sounded like a more consonant-heavy 'Trvus.'

It's sort of like listening to the difference between the native Hawaiian and Alaskan languages – the tropical islanders being much freer with their vowels than their Pacific neighbours to the north.

I wasn't to meet The Princess today; she was off to Cork city for the weekend.

Her archaeologist/breakfast-cook husband was attending to two couples who were sick and injured in the breakfast room of B&B#2 when I arrived. A wiry, good-looking man, he'd added tour guiding to a list of professions that included farming and herding. By the looks of the split foursome, nurse, or possibly 'hangover attendant' was on that tally sheet of professional affiliations as well.

He was surprised to see me so early in the day. I was about to speculate as to the possibility of atmospheric thinning, but it was obvious that his charges were in need of IV bottles of saline solution with an adrenaline drip or an injection of hair of the dog, STAT! He gave me directions to The Cottage with cursory notes as to the operations of the place. The Princess had set everything down pretty well in emails, so I figured I'd just let him get back to his guests/patients.

For the second time that morning, I was handed a key and I headed out the front door to origami myself back into the rental car. A mile later, I pulled into The Cottage drive and realised that I had been handed the key to another caricature version of what I was expecting.

This one, however, I could not swap out in twenty-eight days.

▰ ▰ ▰

There were sheep in the garden. At least there were sheep in the garden.

The photos I'd seen online must have been over a decade old, judging by the growth of the hedges in front of the garden. Where the pictures showed low, knee-high tidy shrubbery, there now stood fully grown windbreaks that obscured The Cottage, the drive and much of the valley behind the property when viewed from the laneway. They nearly grew together above the two-track entry drive into the property. As The Cottage faced the south and east, and local apparent noon was approaching, I took a quick look around and noted how little sunlight it was getting.

Unfolding myself from the car, I considered the height of the front garden forest and The Cottage's orientation to the sun's winter path. Figuring in the spine of rolling hills across the laneway, which ran parallel to the sun's path, and the fact that I was standing near the same latitude line upon which lay the city of Irkustk, Russia (a large city in SIBERIA), I didn't need to tap into my celestial navigation training as a US Coast Guard navigator to conclude that I was going to need to do some hiking if I was going to get my vitamin D this winter. Vitamin D is processed in the body from sunlight and is currently linked to immune health, possibly affecting multiple sclerosis progression and symptoms positively.

The Cottage itself looked sturdy enough. Two-foot-thick stone walls all around in a style that, were it clapboard, might be called a saltbox back in New England.

One drape-darkened window, upstairs and down, framed each side of the tongue-and-groove Dutch door with a small window vent above and another fabric-shaded, middle window on the top floor. Stonework chimneys stood large on each side of The Cottage as two columnar bookends to prevent the two storeys of stone from folding over to one side or the other. A new-looking slate roof would surely keep the weather out.

I hurried myself to the door to see what new additions and changes had been made to the inside in the years since the Internet promotional photos had been taken. I knew that those photos were at least as old as the exterior shots, for I had spied a family picture, framed on the wall at B&B#2. The same toddling boy who was holding himself up by the arm of a slightly blurred piece of print-upholstered furniture that my great-gran would have called a 'Davenport' in the photo was now a strapping young lad of nine or ten and was holding himself up, sans sofa, just fine.

I would have noted, shortly after opening the door and allowing my eyes to adjust to night vision, that, while the lad was no longer a toddler, everything else about The Cottage – E-V-E-R-Y-T-H-I-N-G – was exactly the same as advertised. Every piece of furniture was the same as in the photos, each one placed exactly as it had been posed for what I'm guessing were Kodachrome snapshots, scanned and posted for use as bait to lure mildly disabled Americans searching for a place to pretend they were Irish for a winter.

I would have noted these things shortly after opening the door. But it took me nearly twenty minutes, for I had to make my way around The Cottage – upstairs and down – throwing open windows and the back door just to get some oxygen into the place. The stiff, acrid smell that I immediately feared – from walking into far too many empty and abandoned restaurant kitchens – to be either old deep-fryer grease or evidence of a serious roach problem was actually the stifling aroma of a very old dishwasher-sized oil boiler that heated both water and Cottage via newish-looking radiators. My eyes watered and my nose stung from the offensive air, which was making the same, quick escape that I was now considering.

Drapes pulled back and sunlit fresh air flowing in through the windows, The Cottage began to reveal itself to me. It was rough, no doubt. The one bit of carpeting that ran up the stairs from the ground floor to the first and along a narrow hallway at the back to the bath was dirty and threadbare in places. Cobwebs waved in every corner like ghostly Halloween décor and the windows – both inside and out – looked as though they'd last been washed for the big photo shoot a decade before. Walls showed stains of ancient water leakage and small piles of dusty mortar lay at the foot of each of the stone walls whence it had crumbled.

The Cottage was compact and dirty, but it seemed functional. On the ground floor, the Dutch door opened into the main salon, the largest room, which took up two-thirds of this level, and had once served as the kitchen of the house but was now the living room. The large open-hearth fireplace filled a hefty chunk of the northeast wall. I was excited that it was still adorned with the cast-iron swinging arm used to hang cooking pots and roast of meat. I intended to play with an old French recipe for leg of lamb roasted by hanging it in front of the fire with butcher's twine and setting it a-spin for a couple of hours. Next to the fireplace, at the back of The Cottage, stood that steep and narrow carpeted stairway with a wooden banister leading to the first floor. We would call that the second floor in America and the ground floor the first. As I was in Ireland now, the upstairs was the first floor.

The other third of the ground floor had been walled off and a simple door opened to the residence's current kitchen. It was a relatively modernised room, complete with French-plate stove top and oven (the 'cooker') and a refrigerator of a size that promotes daily walks to the market. There was also a large, country pine dining table surrounded by six dining chairs – not a matching pair among them. The second of the two fireplaces advertised was in this room. A lovely ornamental cast-iron sort of thing, it looked as though it had been salvaged from a Victorian townhouse. Its chimney, however, had been plugged by sticks and stones dropped by rooks to the point of making it too stopped up for all but the most expensive of chimney sweeps. I would not find this out until days later, when the kitchen filled with turf smoke from my first attempt at a kitchen fire.

Green-tiled countertops and backsplash, terracotta-coloured walls, soft timber floors, and knotty pine cabinetry completed the 'look'. Were I to put a design-style label on the colour palette of the room, I'd have a hard time choosing between 'Country Kaleidoscope' and 'Farmhouse Fire-sale'.

The two windowsills at the front of this floor both offered two feet (the depth of the walls) of shelf space. They'd make for extra seating come Christmas, when there would be seven of us in this hobbit-sized space.

At the back was a small utility/storage/mud entry from the back garden. This space was cordoned off by a twin of the kitchen door. Tucked under the stairway, behind another simple-latched door, was a WC. This toilet room was cramped and narrow, with a direct vent to the outside that allowed so much of a breeze into the room that I was a little bit frightened to open the latch for the shaking. I feared there might be a *céilí* in progress.

Up the back staircase and the first floor was all about sleeping.

The largest bedroom was situated over most of the living room. Just as advertised, it held an iron bed, dresser, wardrobe and a decorated pottery sink, hand-thrown by a local potter, I would come to learn. I'd say it's the largest bedroom, but with all that furniture, it looked as much like an antiques storage room as a bedroom. The windows on this floor also had deep sills that might serve well as an alternative way in and out of the bed.

On the kitchen end of the house was a smaller bedroom that I claimed as my own for most of the stay. Three couples would be staying with me over the next three months as well as two sets of women friends who would be forced to share a room. I did the host-ly thing, deciding they would need the space far more than I.

This room also happened to be closest to the upstairs bathroom. Likely the newest room in The Cottage, it featured a 1980s version of an art deco mirror, hung above a pedestal sink. A very deep bathtub fitted with an electric power shower had a lovely window so that you could enjoy the view down to the harbour and (on a clear day) all the way out to the Skellig Islands while washing your 'real estate'. It also allowed the neighbours to monitor water usage from both front and back gardens as well as just about any room on the facing side of their house. I could only guess that my future house guests would find the window notable mostly for the view it allowed the neighbours in rather than the stunning views out.

Both the shower window and the other in the bathroom – with an expansive view past the back garden, down the valley and up the other side to another range of mountain foothills – are the only windows in the entire house without dressing. The view from that second window is absolutely breathtaking and can be enjoyed only from a seated position on the old-fashioned, pull-chain toilet. No

Sheep in the garden shortly after my arrival.

reading materials required in this bog! Between the two bedrooms was a large closet. This closet was furnished with a set of twin bunk beds, a chest of drawers and a spare dining chair. The high ceiling, which, as in the rest of the rooms on this level, went all the way up to the peak of the roof, gave an illusion of much more space than there really was. Were I not to know better, I'd say that two kittens could share this space quite comfortably. We'll call this room the 'sleeping closet'.

The Princess gave me an excellent deal on the place for the entire winter. I was paying per month for the three months, in fact, the same rate she would have charged someone per week for the three weeks around the Christmas holidays. Coping with its 'charming idiosyncrasies' and spending a few hours cleaning and rearranging would be a small price to pay for the bargain.

I scurried about to aerate the place, with my knees in the sink trying to reach the latch of the back kitchen window. The latch was beyond a two-foot sill so I abandoned the effort after nearly impaling myself on the tap. That's when I spotted a small flock of a half dozen or so sheep in the back garden. They must have been some of the pregnant ewes Your Man said he'd brought down from the high fields for the winter. There they were, right there in my back garden, eating grass and paying no attention whatsoever to the interloper kneeling in the kitchen sink.

Sure the place needed some cleaning up – and 'some' is obviously a result of three months of positive memories shading the truth. To paraphrase the song, things we don't like to recall, we can decide to forget, or something like that. No, it wasn't everything I had hoped for nor expected. And absolutely it hit me between the eyes that my first house guests were arriving in fewer than four days.

But at least there were SHEEP in the garden!

7

Shopping as it Should Be

UNPACKED, I REALISED that the 'warm flannel sheets for ye' and 'lots of towels, don't you worry' that The Princess had promised were nowhere to be found. Neither was Your Man when I called into B&B#2 (and I had no idea where B&B#1 was) to inquire about the same. He may have taken his guests-cum-medical charges to the hospital or to the pub; I still couldn't figure which they'd needed. Fortuitously, in The Town, the same hardware store into which I had wandered to stock up on cleaning supplies, air fresheners and sheep dip was also a fully stocked housewares outlet. Not only did I find the hammers, trowels, chisels and scrapers for the light housekeeping ahead, but also sheets, towels, lace café curtains and a tea service plus a full selection of furniture and artwork. It was all crammed into the brightly lit 113 square feet of the shop.

I grew up with a store not completely unlike this one in my neighbourhood. It was nothing like this at all, but it was not completely unlike. I would tail behind my Da to the local hardware when he was looking for a particular penny-size nail or a bolt-screw-or-fastener of a certain job, and the owner himself would know exactly what we needed, where it was and the price to charge (or to make up, as I don't ever remember seeing a price tag or sign anywhere).

Your Man at this establishment gave me the same service as well as advising me of the time of the next tide, the days of the week that the fishmonger's cart was open, and which was the best pub in The Town for Guinness – 'the closest one what's opened at the time', by the way.

The very few things I couldn't obtain via the hardware I picked up at the local SuperValu grocery and heard over the store intercom system for the first time what would later be a catchphrase for the market: 'Now, customers, that's shopping as it should be!'

By the time I'd stocked the larder, the fridge and the cleaning cupboard, bought coal, turf briquettes and kindling sticks for the fireplace, and topped up the skate-ball bag's tank with petrol, I'd improved the local economy and lightened my purse by a factor near equivalent to my round-trip airfare.

After the shopping spree, there was just enough of my exchanged currency for a quiet dinner. The day's travel and the white-tornado cleaning at The Cottage had left just enough of the loan-shark drug in my system for the same.

It's a dinner I'd been looking forward to for months.

That night with my sister and brother – the one that had begun with 'too much wine' back in February – we dined in a mildly posh little place on the main street. The chef who owned the place was very talented, and with little more than a glance at our orders figured we knew food and invited me back into her kitchen for a tour.

Chefs being who we are, one thing led to another … I'm fairly sure she sent twice as much free food compared to our actual order. I'm absolutely sure that we made up for it on the bar tab.

As is likely to happen when you think-dream-plan (obsess?) about something for months, you set yourself up for disappointment. The place was shuttered.

I'd forgotten that it was Sunday night and couldn't fault Your One for taking a night off. Across the street was another fine-looking establishment, if a little more 'masculine' in its appearance – a 'meat and two veg' kind of place, and they were at least open. I sidled up to the bar along the side of the room of Miller's Restaurant, away from most of the tables, and ordered the barman to pull the first pint of Guinness of my stay.

Now, be it known, the process of building a proper pint can take more pages than my publishers would allow but I will say this: while it may take as long as ten minutes, this allows for the niceties long forgotten by all but a few of the world's drinkers. You get to know your publican, and he or she, you. Histories of the establishment, your family, their family, the town and the county can be exchanged. By the time the last of the creamy head has settled, you've likely had a chance to assess the menu (if it's food you're looking for) or debate the parliamentary system of government and most of *The Origin of Species*.

Ah, but it is one of the great joys in life if built well … and this pint was built very well.

During the construction process, I learned that Your One hadn't simply closed for the night. She'd closed the place for good and was selling. You see, she'd just had a baby girl.

The bartender didn't actually tell me she'd had a baby girl. Rather, in lyric form beyond the reach of even the best writer he stated, 'Oh, sure. Didn't she have t'ree magpie round her place in the spring?'

My extensive knowledge of the winged life of the island coupled with an intensive study of local children's poetry put me right onto the path he was laying out. Well, that and the lost-at-sea look on my face caused him to recite the verse about magpies for me:

> One for sorrow,
> Two for joy,
> Three for a girl,
> Four for a boy,
> Five for silver,
> Six for gold,
> Seven for a secret never to be told.

While we talked of avian prediction prowess and how his father had started the restaurant decades before, I flipped through the menu.

'And it's lamb shank for the Roast Special tonight,' added Your Man.

The foreshank of lamb (or beef, or veal, or pork, etc.) is a flavourful piece of meat that requires long, moist cooking under low to moderate heat with a touch of acid in order to cook the sinewy meat while simultaneously rendering collagen into soft, lip-smacking gelatin. Too much heat and the muscle fibres toughen beyond hope of ever sawing through with knife or teeth. Too little browning at the beginning of the process and the cooking liquid never takes on the full, rich flavour required to match the bold meat. Too slow and the meat dries out – even though cooked in liquid – before tendon and connective tissue give up their gelatinous goodness.

The oldie-but-not-mouldy, almost clubby feel of the house made me feel as if a lamb shank was exactly the kind of dish I should try. Without a further look at the menu, I decided on the Roast Special and took a long and very satisfying draw from the creamy pint of black that had finally settled itself in the glass in front of me.

The braised lamb shank was perfection, tender but not fall-apart, unctuous but not sticky, fragrant but not too gamey. Truly the chef was an artist who knew his way around a piece of meat.

When he found out that I came from Seattle, where his girlfriend (whom he'd met in Dublin but was currently working in New York, of course) was raised, Your Man offered me a glass of port to toast the familiarity. I'm sure he also saw it as a wise investment. It was the icing on an impeccable country meal, and I was now sure to bring in every one of my fifteen scheduled house guests at least once.

The quality of the lamb and its cookery brought to mind the fun I hoped to have with the local produce. I'd remembered there being a butcher in The Town so I asked Your Man about the quality of the place.

'Isn't it from Himself what you just ate came?' I was going to have to get used to the fact that many of my questions would be answered not only with the raised inflection of the Valley Girl vernacular but with an actual question mark.

The butcher where locals buy their rashers and chops is also the finest source of meat in the county, he tells me.

I made a quick 'I've arrived safely' call to family in America from the same phone box where Billy had taken a transatlantic scolding for calling home and not recognising his wife's voice over his daughter's, then I dragged myself back up the hill, well fed and watered. By now it was obvious that the neuropathy meds were wearing off and the loan shark was at the door. On Monday I would have to pay the bastard back for the advance with interest but, all in all, it had been a great first day.

I would spend the next day recovering because another long drive awaited me for Tuesday, when it was prearranged for me to drive to Athy in County Kildare. I'd been looking forward to this since 15 July, the day she was born.

On Tuesday I would get my puppy!

8

Peg O' My Heart

THE FULL STORY OF HOW I came to get my puppy was printed in a popular article I wrote for *Killarney* magazine. The widely successful magazine folded not long after.

I grew up with dogs ('dogs' to use the vernacular – they were actually all bitches) in the house. The random times I've come across the couple of old family snapshots I have of the first dog, they still bring mist to my eyes. She was a Border collie/German shepherd mix we called Boofy, as her puppy barks sounded like 'boof !' rather than 'woof.' We got Boofy in my first grade year and she died while I was away on my first Coast Guard ship. A good long life.

We had others, but Boofy was the dog every boy wants; she wanted to play when I did, she'd rest her head on me when I was ill, and she'd look at me the way only a dog can when I was doing or about to do something really, really stupid.

I'd wanted a dog for a long time, but both my professional schedule and that of my former wife, Sheri, when we were married, would have made for the kind of life I've seen far too many dogs in America have. I would not get a pet while I was working twelve-or-more-hour days in kitchens or travelling over 200,000 miles a year for work. Nor would I leave the responsibility to Sheri. Besides, I'm glad we didn't. Being card-carrying members of the child-free, we would have found the post-divorce custody arrangements difficult at best.

We'd often talked about getting dogs – two bitches, Welsh corgis maybe. We'd name the first Peg, after my great-gran (of 'let's call furniture funny names' fame) who was really named Violet but my great-gramp called her Peg after the song 'Peg O' My Heart', which was popular when they were courting in 1913. The other would be called Sadie, after Sheri's grandmother, the most irreverent grandmother anyone could wish for.

I decided not long after my February return to Seattle and setting this move into motion that I had reached a time and place in my life and my MS where a dog would be a good fit – a perfect fit, really. Now I needed the perfect breed.

My search for that 'perfect' breed for me had taken nearly fifteen years. Obviously, if I were to get my newest companion while in Ireland, she would have to be an Irish breed. That was easy. Which of the famed Irish breeds to choose, however?

There is the ennobled Kerry Blue Terrier, the loyal and beautiful Irish Setter, and its cousin, the Red and White Setter. The kinky brown Water Spaniel, the Glen of Imaal Terrier, and the very, very large Irish Wolfhound all have their draw – save perhaps the wolfhound, which I love but would not make a cosy flatmate back in my home in Seattle.

It was, after all, a puppy that I searched for. I was looking for the dog that would forever live in *Tír na nÓg*. What I came to understand through my research was that I was in need of an Irish Soft-Coated Wheaten Terrier.

And that was that.

Finding such a puppy in Ireland, however, while still living in Seattle … now that was a task far easier than I'd expected.

Say what you will about the temporary nature of the world's society of today, but were it not for the Internet, my hunt would have taken months, not hours. As many things do, my hunt started with a venture to Google.com. After only a few moments, I was e-troduced to an auburn-haired lass called Helen and the Newkdara Kennels in a small town in County Kildare that isn't far from Portlaoise – another town that figures vaguely into my family's past. Upon contacting Your One by phone, I asked how long she had been involved with the breed. Her answer was what I was now beginning to find quite typically Irish.

'Oh, not that long, really, maybe fourteen or fifteen years,' she quipped.

'Fifteen years, not "long"?!' I pondered aloud.

'Well, my family has been breeding Wheatens for three generations.'

Come to find out, Helen's great-grandfather was breeding Soft-Coated Wheaten Terriers even prior to their acceptance into either the Irish or UK Kennel Clubs in the early part of the last century.

Ah, the Internet …

Helen, as luck would have it, had a dam that would be having her pups in late July, making them ready for homing upon my arrival early in November.

While she was to offer me the pick of the litter, I think it can be unanimously agreed that mine was not to be the typical course of choosing a puppy. We started a weekly email exchange of photos and personality updates of the three females of the litter of seven the day they were born.

By the time week eight came around, I was still up in the air as to which of the three females from the litter would be my partner for whatever trouble we might find in the wilds of Kerry. Once that week's photo came across cyberspace, however, it was as if the decision had been made for me.

In one of the photos of the electronic packet I opened, a little pup stood while the other two sat looking out from my computer screen. Her wee tail blocked out the letter 'J' in a sporting headline that was stuffed into a corner behind the three. What was supposed to read 'YOU JOSE!' – apparently calling out a footballer who hadn't been (and I'm only guessing here) named after an Irish relative – now appeared to read 'YOU LOSE.'

I was hers! And today, she was to be mine.

Only getting one puppy, I decided to call her Sadie for short, but her full registered name was to be Newkdara Sadie Peg O' My Heart, in honour of the aforementioned grandmothers.

I'd earlier warned of the dangers of making time-to-distance judgments without ample knowledge of the routes. Consulting the new *Ordnance Survey Ireland Road Atlas* (purchased at the hardware along with sugar, bread, towels, bed sheets and a lovely bar of verbena soap), I decided to use the green or National primary routes as much as possible, which constituted all but about 30 miles of the 150-mile journey. I figured I could average 50 miles per hour by using these National primary routes. If I left bright and early, I could be there by lunch, pick up Herself and be back in time to test her herding abilities with the garden sheep for a few hours before dark.

Let's just say that my warning came as a result of this hard-fought lesson and leave it at that.

By the time Little Miss Sadie and I arrived back at The Cottage I had been on the road for over twelve hours, she had wet the fleece liner Helen had laid down in her travel kennel (just as the prescient breeder had forecast), and I was swearing off car travel in the country for all but emergency medical procedures or evacuations – if, for instance, I needed to outrun any potential tidal waves that might come our way in the next three months.

9

Of Course ...

IT IS NOT UNCOMMON, or intended, for me to slip into an Irish accent when drinking around locals or in 'irish' (small 'i') pubs in America. I don't mean to speak like the poser I know I am when I do it. It just happens.

At a late-night chipper I ordered fried plaice and curried chips while Sadie, fed, watered, relieved and barricaded in the kitchen, acclimated herself to her new surroundings. That's when I was caught 'doing' the accent, and I hadn't had a single drop since my first night.

'Where'ye from then?' asked the sophisticated-looking hostess/cashier/waitress/cook who I would later learn was also the owner.

'Uhhhhh, I live in Seattle.' I backed it off as much as I could without sounding like John Wayne.

'Sure then, but where'ye from, HERE?'

I suppose I could have said I was renting The Cottage from The Princess and explained the whole story but determined that the fewer words I could use in the interaction, the more likely it was that I could make it most of the way to the skate-ball bag before she called all the neighbours out to point at me and laugh.

'The family's from Fermanagh,' I said, only stretching the truth by about 300 years.

'Ah! I thought so. I'm from Cavan!' says she. 'I thought I heard a northern twang, so.'

How, I wondered, could the version of the accent with which I'd played since I was a boy – the one a pint of black could so easily induce – how could that accent be the proper accent whence my people come?

Coincidence? Luck? Genetic memory?

I didn't really want to take the time to figure it out. I wasn't absolutely sure Your One wasn't having me on for a laugh. But she was for real.

We talked of her mother still in Cavan, the fact that she drove all the way there and back every fortnight to visit her, my new puppy, the current price of wool and all of the other requisite niceties called for by proper social edict when waiting for the curry sauce to heat and breaded fish to boil in oil. She dug a small piece of smoked salmon from the back of a small refrigerated cooler and offered it as a 'welcome to the neighbourhood' treat for Sadie.

We parted the best of friends, and I didn't have to look over my shoulder more than twice to see if the neighbours were gathering.

There must be something about the front door to The Cottage, because for the second time in three days, upon opening, I was struck with a bolt of offensive aroma strong enough to stun a boer goat.

Newkdara Sadie Peg O' My Heart apparently had a nervous digestive system. Most puppies are homed at around eight or nine weeks. The extra month (along with the training and family bonding Helen had afforded Sadie once we knew she was Sadie) must have added to the stress of being assaulted by my northern twang for the entirety of our epic journey back to The Town.

She sat now, shaking in the corner of the kitchen and looking at me through a stinking haze that emanated from the near entirety of the floor. I don't know if she thought she was to be reprimanded for the accident, or if she was frightened of the whole move or a combination of those and other factors known only to dogs. Whatever the cause, the first order of business was to take Herself up to the bathtub and give her a good wash.

I towelled her in front of the heat of a dying turf fire, where she fell asleep before she was completely dry.

Leaving her to rest, I did what every puppy owner (and I'm guessing, parent) has done far more than once. I cleaned the mess, sanitised the room and then threw away my dinner, now more than an hour cold.

✐ ✐ ✐

I wish I could report that a calm and restful night's sleep greeted both Sadie and me. It would have made the remainder of the morning's follies far closer to tolerable.

Herself wasn't used to sleeping in a crate, the house-training method I had settled upon, or maybe the Brooks Brothers Italian wool sweater I used to replace her wetted fleece wasn't comfortable. Whatever the reason, she whimpered and whined herself to sleep and then back awake again for most of the night. By the time it was 6.30 a.m. and what we used to call 'Civil Twilight' back in the day lightened the sky, neither of us was rested, but we both had to pee.

I dashed as quickly as my weakened limbs would carry me from my cold bed – I'd yet to master the oil boiler for heat – to the colder loo and back, then slipped boots onto my sockless feet. A big jumper, pyjama bottoms, and cap finished my ensemble, and I suited up Herself with her American import collar and lead for introduction to the sheep in the garden.

Back and forth across, around and through every part of the front garden we traipsed. 'Terrier' comes from the root 'of the earth', and that is firmly where Sadie's nose was locked. She wandered about smelling the stones, the dirt, the skate-ball bag's tyres, the fences and shrubbery. She flinched a bit when the sheep caught her eye (oh, and they were warily watching her!), but she didn't back down from their bleating and threatening stamping of the ground.

Instead, she looked up at me – the first time I had felt her seeing me, like a child who could newly focus – and cocked her head the way we all know puppies can, looking back and forth from the sheep to me as if to ask if these were her sheep. 'Mine? All mine … REALLY? For me?'

Then, she finally peed.

✦ ✦ ✦

The comedy of what happened next was surely evident in the moment, to those who were unfortunate enough to witness our morning as it unfolded. For Sadie and me, however, the next several hours were the coming to life of childhood nightmares. At least they were my childhood nightmares. Sadie was in for an introduction to The Town.

The big, old Dutch door of The Cottage was heavy and well hung, and even when the fireplace was drawing like a blacksmith's forge, it could be closed with one hand. On that still morning, with nothing but a few dying embers from the coal that had dried Herself after her required previous night's shower on the grate, the door had closed and latched itself behind us upon our exit to pee with the sheep. I reached into my pants pocket for the key I'd retrieved from B&B#2, only to remember I wasn't wearing pants, only pyjama bottoms.

Though she was young, Sadie was – and is – a very smart dog.

Helen had begun lead training her as soon as we knew her to be 'Sadie', and she learned quickly. Once finished up with her morning piddle, she knew the routine should continue back into The Cottage, where she would await her breakfast. The look in her eyes had changed from excitement about the sheep-toys I'd offered up and her little mind had moved on to more important things: warmth, food, perhaps a kip while her new Da built her another one of those wonderfully bright and warm fires but first, 'You have to open the door, now …'

I'd of course been vigilant the night before to secure all doors, windows, hatches and portholes before retiring. Probably overly vigilant for the bucolic environs of The Cottage where The Town butted up against miles of farm fields and sheep pastures. Certainly I'd been overly vigilant for our current circumstances: clad in a hotchpotch of day and night clothes with no visible ingress that didn't call for later reglazing and extensive explanations. We had one key. It was in my pants on the chair, next to the bed, in the upstairs bedroom, all behind a very locked door. It looked like Herself and I were in for a morning constitutional before our breakfast.

There were no paved footpaths along the laneway. In fact each side of the road was paralleled by two-foot-deep drainage gullies, which all but met the tarmacadam. We headed down the rather steep hill to The Town, both of our heads bowed – Sadie's in order for her sniffer to pick up the new scents that met her every step, and mine in shame and embarrassment that I was living out the chimera of attending school half-clad. It was, fortunately, early enough in the morning that we encountered neither a single person nor car until we reached the heart of The Town. Using several of the side streets and alleys Billy and I had stumbled through to a phone box and back, we managed to find our way, triumphantly, to the door of B&B#2, detected only by the occasional neighbourhood Border collie and a sleepy cat cleaning herself in the morning sun on a doorstep. Sadie had taken keen interest in the feline, as she'd been raised with several cats at Helen's home. I picked her up and carried the puppy for the last few blocks. The last thing I wanted to be doing that morning, aside from walking through the streets of my new – if only temporary – home town in my pyjamas, was chasing a dog chasing a cat through the streets and gardens of my new neighbours' homes dressed more for the night before than for the morning after.

Standing before the door to B&B#2, I congratulated myself, and Sadie, on our uneventful resolution to our morning situation. Not many can say that they've traversed the better part of a busy little town in their pyjamas unnoticed. A quick explanation and we'd be given a lift back up the hill to our adopted little country home and our day would be back on track – perhaps even better for the story.

No one answered the bell.

I was beginning to get that look again from Sadie as I led her around the townhouse-cum-bed and breakfast, peering into each lace-curtain-trimmed window and finding nothing to raise hope of a quick resolution.

The reason no one answered the bell, for all I could garner, was that there was no one in the place. All the tables in the breakfast room had been reset after the other morning's medical breakfast. There was neither sound nor light nor anything, really, to evidence occupation. The sun, which had been behind the rim of low mountains when we arrived, was now above the horizon someplace and the day had become fully lit.

Thinking first of the phone box as a means of getting a hold of my landlords, I came to the rolling realisation that my current state of dress afforded me neither of the two requisites to using said technology to our benefit: 1) As was the case with my pyjamas pockets lacking a house key, neither did they contain coin. 2) Equally blaring was the fact that pockets, nor jumper nor brain, for that matter, contained the numbers I'd have to dial in order to reach my key-masters.

Herself, it should be noted, was chosen to be my Sadie in great part because of her personality. While it was only weekly emailed files of photographs that I was judging, her inclination to be an 'observer' of situations struck me. In one photograph, Helen called the pack of seven pups to her on their first foray into the garden without their mammy. While some pups beelined straight for their surrogate, two others appeared to wander toward whatever happened to catch their big brown eyes, and one had turned its back to the situation, completely. Sadie, however, had plunked herself down at the back of the formation as if to see what might be the outcome of each possibility.

So was the case this morning.

Sadie found a tuft of grass no larger than my fist struggling up through a crack in the footpath and plunked herself down on her bum. She was no doubt exhausted from her previous eighteen-hour experience and maybe even sensed that I was rolling the options and ticking each off for their lack of possibility and/or plausibility. Her head moved in tandem with mine as it rolled up the lane and back, up the side of B&B#2 and down. It was probably I who first cocked my head 30 degrees in rather canine fashion as I soaked my brain in possibility, hoping to reach a common sense resolution.

It was from that same, seated position on her claimed bit of grass that she looked down on me in the gutter between footpath and lane.

As oft happens with my version of MS, my mind sometimes forgets that its constituents are no longer able to answer in sequential manner. When the brightest flicker of hope I could foretell required my eyes, head, shoulders, torso, hips, legs and feet to move fluidly from right to left in order to face the direction of my intent, the signals left my brain and hit one of those corroded bits of wiring. Flailing like an untended fire hose, I crumpled to the deck and learned something new about my companion.

It was neither with shock nor alarm that she stood and padded over to me at lead's end. She stopped at the edge of the footpath, looked both ways, jumped on my chest, and began wildly licking my face. I'm not sure which was moving faster, her tongue or her tail and therefore, by extension, her whole back half. Pure joy exuded from every ounce of my puppy and it infused me like a bag of corticosteroids with energy and purpose.

There are some things that happen in Ireland that go beyond explanation. It's best just to accept that things happen there, for reasons unknown, that don't happen elsewhere. Lifting myself and my pup up from the pavement, I spied something leaning against a hedgerow that stopped at the edge of B&B#2. I didn't recall at the time – nor do I to this day – seeing the blackthorn walking stick tucked neatly between an iron gate and the hedge of less-than-manicured laurel, but there it was. With every intention of returning the stick to its place after I was able to replace it with my own walking aid, I crawled from the lane and used the blackthorn to hoist myself to standing. With my leg now supported, my plan gelling and my face freshly wetted, I set forth down the block, dragging my left side like a cartoon monster. I wore a confident expression, as if I were not in my PJs and had no doubts that my plan would actually work.

In front of the SuperValu I had used to stock my cupboards just a few days prior, there was a quaint old hitching post and ring. One might be forgiven for assuming that it served no real purpose and was simply a reminder of days gone by. (In just about any American town, that would be the case.) Over the course of my stay, however, I would see any number of farm animals, from a horse and donkeys to a tired old ram, tied to its ring. On this day it served as a convenient hitch for young Sadie as I shook off every last remaining scrap of pride I'd managed to hold onto after my spill into the gutter and slowly entered the market.

Sadie, once again, curled her tail under her bum and sat to observe.

The morning was turning out to be a case of one 'of course' after another. Of course I locked myself out of the house. Of course I had to walk down to The Town without a cane. Of course I fell after such a long walk, and of course there was a walking stick perched for my use. Now, of course the woman working the only open register in the market was the manager. Of course she knew The Princess. Of course she knew the phone number and of course, by the time this had all transpired, the landlord had gone to B&B#2 to make his guests breakfast. I'm guessing I should add that of course the manager and the few people wandering in and out for morning coffee and a newspaper noted that there was a new American in town who liked to roam around, pyjama-clad, asking for favours.

My plan had worked. Your Man let us in and had the spare key ready to hand off by the time we arrived at the door. What didn't work was my assumption that we'd get a quick lift up the hill to The Cottage. He was late making breakfast for his guests and couldn't spare a moment. Sadie and I, along with our newly acquired cane and key, were left to exit the far more awake town than we had entered on foot.

It is fair if you have wondered how a man living with multiple sclerosis and wearing PJs could hike nearly a mile down into and around The Town at all, let alone in such cold conditions. You see, while it might seem counterintuitive at first, cold can be a boon to one living with MS, as was the case here. Not for everyone and not all of the time, even for those of us who find some cold helpful.

Heat is the real enemy.

If you think about a computer server room of an office building or even your home electronics, you'll note that there are fans or extensive air conditioning systems to keep the wiring cool. It's actually to keep the electrons that are moving around cool so the system doesn't overheat. When a person with MS experiences a fever or a particularly hot day, our 'electrical systems' (central nervous system) can misfire, and many of our symptoms will relapse in what is known as a pseudo exacerbation.

When I say 'pseudo,' I don't mean these symptoms (usually a return or heightening of existing symptoms) are not real, but rather, they are not symptoms of a new attack on the brain. It is more like aggravating an old injury which has semi-healed and will get no better.

The night had been cold and our Cottage walls not yet warmed to their new residents. The morning was cold, and quite frankly, I wasn't what one would call bundled for the elements. This uncomfortable cascade of climate and clothing had allowed me to cover the distance into The Town without much trouble. The exertion of the walk coupled with the stresses of the morning were beginning to work against me, as was the rising warmth of the sun as we proceeded back up our hill.

Even with numerous stops to rest, which I was able to disguise as pauses for Sadie to smell her new surrounds, I'd be lying if I said that getting back up the hill was easy. By the time we passed our overgrown hedgerow and reached the end of the two-track drive, both puppy and papa were pooped.

While Sadie dispatched her morning (now nearly afternoon) meal, I could only muster the energy to assemble toast and tea for myself.

We retired to the main room, where I had to start fresh with a fire on the grate, all of the early morning embers having gone grey and cold. And there we stayed for the remainder of the day. Re-stoking the fire and making more tea were about all the tasks I could muster. Sadie seemed perfectly contented with our day of recuperation, and after her long morning trek, she made only the shortest work of any calling nature had for her.

I poached an amazingly fresh hen's egg to go with my evening tea and we ascended the stairs early. The Cottage was still quite cold, and though a warm bed sounded far more inviting than the icy sheets I was about to part, I hoped that another bracing night would repair the damage we'd done. I had, after all, to set my alarm for 2 a.m. so that we could fold ourselves into the skate-ball bag, drive to Shannon, and collect our first house guests – my parents.

10

Rashers and Sausages and Pudding, Oh, My!

SADIE'S FIRST UNCRATED excursion with her new Da was to be a six-hour round trip with over half of it occurring in the dark of night. She settled herself into the back window of the car, behind the headrests. Though she was much larger than the dime-store variety, she looked not unlike a bobble-headed ornament, lying as she was above the back seats. Though I'd been on these roads before, it was my first go at navigating the frosty country roads with nothing more than cockeyed headlights to guide my way.

We stopped a few times along the route to see if Herself had to empty but she seemed much more interested in the pee-mail other beasts had left for her to discover than depositing her own urine-posts in return. A 24-hour filling station that sported a very modern deli kitchen happened to be in our path to Shannon, and I suddenly realised that the last real meal I'd had was thirty-six hours prior. I was famished.

Once again I was privy to one of those fortunes that seem to happen with greater frequency in Ireland. The overnight keeper of said station had fallen ill the day before, I was advised by the manager as she assembled my breakfast plate. The quaint Kerry woman who covered his shift not only managed the business but was also the deli's cook. Had Your Man not contracted whatever ailment that kept him from his shift, the cook would have been still in her bed and I without the opportunity of a hot meal and a lovely conversation.

After devouring a sausage roll still juicy from the oven and a rasher sandwich on brown bread sliced from a fresh loaf, I was filled, the skate-ball bag was filled, and Sadie finally emptied – on a small strip of lawn at the edge of the station's tarmacadam. We set off as the sky lit from blue-black to steel.

* * *

Were I to take a mental spade to it, I'd have to dig for a while until I found the one benefit to gathering visitors at such an early hour. That advantage would rest in the opening hours of Irish pubs.

The last time my Da and I drove the road from Shannon to Kerry together (along with my mother on that trip as well), we had made reservations at a small bed and breakfast (owned by a locally famous uilleann pipe maker) on the north side of The Other Larger Town. The distance had been relatively short and the hour much later, for they had stopped first in Dublin on a continuing flight. We took the scenic route (funny, really, to think one route more scenic than another in this beautiful part of the island) and were able to find an open public house in short order.

Little pleases me more than seeing my Da tucked in next to a glowing grate with a pint glass half-full of thick, black Guinness, streaks of creamy head clinging to its sides like wisps of seaweed marking the tide on an ancient pier. Were we to pass an open establishment, we'd no doubt stop, and things being as they were, the hours would pass, and we'd be returning to The Cottage in the same darkness I'd left it. That's just how things happen in this corner of Ireland.

As Da describes it, 'Pubs aren't "bars". They're like communal living rooms for a place. You go in there after work or after supper or after whatever to talk about the day, the local politics, or the price of wool.'

You can see why a pint with Da can take up an afternoon. Sadie greeted my parents with all the enthusiasm one would expect from an Irish puppy. Rather than making herself too familiar with them, however, she tucked herself back into her spot behind the headrests and seemed to listen to our conversations intently. Until, of course, we pulled out of Shannon's car park. At which point she laid her head on her paws, let out a sweet, nasal sigh and drifted fast to sleep.

🐦 🐦 🐦

Sadie and I had taken the coast road out of The Town, so I decided to make it a loop on our return and take the mountain road home. We'd driven this route the last time my parents had visited Ireland, and I remembered how much they had liked the drive. In actuality, I guess, what they'd really liked about the drive were the stories they were able to tell their friends afterward.

The mountain road is one of those that you hear stories about from people who come back from tours around Ireland. You hear of the harrowing turns and twists of the road, how the stone walls that separate pasture from path can jump out and snatch a wing mirror, and the inevitable tale of two cars meeting on roads so narrow that one driver is forced to back up hundreds of yards in order to allow the other to pass. All of the above is assuredly true. The mountain road does wind its way up one side of the spine that backs The Town. Though European Union funds have widened many dangerous roads in Kerry, this mountain road isn't one of them. But it must be said that the only time I've ever seen anyone back up (or down) the mountain road, they were visitors in rental cars.

Locals just know how to navigate these situations.

First, when driving around the long, sweeping bends that many country roads afford, it is important to look well ahead of your next turn to see what oncoming traffic may present itself. Focusing only on the few hundred yards directly ahead is a rather selfish act of driving when you consider that the narrow strips of tarmac are indeed – no matter that they may be narrower than one's driveway back in the States – shared space. As in few places on earth, each has an equally shared responsibility in squeezing past the other.

Maybe, too, the mountain road is a metaphor for how I've begun to live my life as I get my heart around the idea of living with MS.

So often, as I lived and worked and played in my former life, my gaze was stopped at or by the next curve in the road. So much life was happening all around me, just as so much beauty envelops each bend in an Irish country road. Before, it was easy to live from point to point, turn to turn. Now, while the cascade of 'what if … then I would' could send me sliding off the edge of my new path, I look farther down my road and see shared responsibility in my days.

One cannot dwell on the 'what ifs' of life. I have found, however, that two or three 'then I woulds' help me to sit comfortably in the driver's seat of my new existence without either a) white-knuckling the passage or b) gazing so far ahead that I miss the beauty all around (or worse, end up in a ditch alongside my road).

Others who might be along for the ride may also feel more comfortable knowing that we've seen the potential obstacles in time to adjust our course and speed in order to meet them at a time and place of intention and purpose. At least that's what I like to think I've learned of life and driving on Irish roads. And as if on cue, a car hauling a trailer with a ram behind appeared about a half mile ahead, and on the next bend, a wide(ish) spot on the left, I nudged over to wait his passing.

Sometimes my road is extra narrow and the passing traffic of MS makes if feel like I'll never be able to continue my journey. Today, however, it really was just a car, just a trailer, and just a ram for which I must alter my course. We were soon once again climbing the mountain.

* * *

While the 'rents unpacked and Sadie looked on in their room, I drove myself into The Town.

Your Man behind the bar at my welcome dinner had spoken so highly of the local butcher that I could no longer suppress my professional curiosity. Also, as I was now in possession of my own cane, I felt it appropriate to return the walking stick left for me by the fairies to the hedgerow outside B&B#2. To drive the short distance was a very

'American' thing to do, but I'd not fully recovered from the prior day's ramble.

Besides, I'd already made quite the impression on the few people who saw me in my pyjamas (and the scores whom I anticipated had been regaled with the tale). There was no need to be known not only as the crazy tourist who walked his dog wearing pyjamas but also the loon who carried two walking sticks around with him.

I careened the skate-ball bag around a sharp corner that angled me right in front of the building and pulled up in the very spot to which I had tumbled in front of Sadie just one day earlier. Looking around, I placed the old blackthorn stick right where it had been left for me. I spied no onlookers and so whispered '*Go raibh maith agaibh*' into the bushes and tipped my cap.

Okay, what I really said was, 'Thanks a million' to whomever – or whatever really – had placed the stick for me to find in my time of need. It was only later in my trip that I began to assimilate some of the Irish phrases that one still hears a fair good bit of the time in Kerry.

I'd found the spot for parking and wasn't but a few blocks from the butcher's shop, so I decided to simply walk from there. With cane in hand, cap on head and the muffler my former wife had knitted me for the trip wrapped thrice around, I stepped off toward The Butcher. My ensemble also included moleskin trousers, a turtleneck, Harris Tweed jacket and low-cut L.L. Bean gumshoes. Save for the shoes, I looked (or at least thought I looked) the part of a farmer, come to town.

I had every intention of letting my parents take me to dinner at Miller's, my new-found establishment of local food and gossip, so I didn't plan to load up on anything too extensive this trip. In fact, two of the three shelves in my small refrigerator were already filled (milk for coffee and tea, buttermilk for making bread, butter and yogurt) and that left very little space for multi-day storage. I thought I'd just pick up the meats needed to build a traditional Irish breakfast for their first morning in The Cottage.

As I opened the butcher's door, a small bell rang to announce my arrival. Not that the alarm was needed. I turned from closing the portal and could see just about every bit of the shop and workspace from where I stood. 'Cramped' wouldn't accurately describe the place. 'Efficient' would be closer to the truth. Everything had a place and everything was in its white-tiled place. Knives hung exactly where one would need them on the well-worn, thick wooden butcher's table. The roll of wrapping paper was the perfect distance from the scales and the cash box at the end of the display case nearest the exit. There was no cash register in the shop; the orders were totalled by hand with a pencil on the wrapping of one of your selections.

While the space behind the case was impeccably thought out by someone who had obviously spent enough time there to know the flow of things, the area for customers was, while impeccably clean, quite tight. Much of the space was taken up with a self-service case of local eggs, cellophane-wrapped rashers, and a few other local products at the end of the room. On the wall parallel to the butcher's case were shelves of Kerry condiments, etc. Thus the five customers present (two women and two men, I being the fifth) along with the three men behind the counter put the shop at about maximum capacity.

The smells of the shop were what every chef wants to smell at a butcher's. The fresh, sweet smell of fat mingled with the mineral tones of blood and meat. Cool and copper, it's the kind of smell you might get swirling a particularly well-crafted Malbec in your glass. It also smelled clean without smelling 'cleaned' – no chemical odour under or over the fresh and very local meats. The only hint of smells foreign was not foreign at all, really. The slightest whiff of damp wool layered above it all, but I expected that was from the attire of the customers rather than the animals whence it came.

Busy as the custom was, I was greeted by each one of them. '*Céad míle fáilte*' said a distinguished man in a starched white lab coat and a white paper fedora who waived his sixteen-inch butcher's knife at me in welcome before dispatching slices from the most incredible looking pork loin I'd ever seen.

'Hiya?' said a thin, slightly younger butcher with salt and pepper hair under his matching hat.

An assortment of nods, 'Hiyas?' and a 'Good mornin'' or two came from the congregation at the altar of meat.

From the far end of the room, through a doorway sans door – in the part of the shop where resided the modern tools of the trade like a bandsaw, sausage emulsifier and stuffer as well as large hooks from a rail that ran along the ceiling – boomed the voice of the third butcher.

'WELCOME!' he said to me in a distinctly Scottish accent and, 'Make room for the lad. There's plenty of lamb for everyone today,' to my fellow carnivores as he hoisted the carcass from which he must have been intending to fill our orders (and that of many others, by the size of it).

The imposing ginger-haired Scot washed his hands and dried them before coming out to shake my hand in welcome. He then re-washed and began helping the next customer.

'You're the lad from America then … that's let The Cottage from The Princess?' As he addressed me, he used a long, thin hook to lift a particular piece of lamb's liver indicated by an older woman who'd stepped up to be served. (He, of course, didn't call her 'The Princess,' but as I hope to re-enter the town on speaking terms one day, we'll just go with that.)

'Aye,' said I. 'I plan to spend the winter.' I wasn't all that surprised that word had spread, but wondered which of my follies – the barman, the woman at the chipper, or my pyjamaed parade – had informed the Highlands' butcher of my coming. 'Your Man from Miller's said you might stop in,' chimed in the older, distinguished butcher, as if reading my wonder.

'And you've already a pup for your stay, too?' asked the woman whose family would dine on the liver now being wrapped.

'A Fermanagh man, are we to understand?' chimed in the salt-n-pepper butcher.

No need to wonder which source. All seemed to have been utilised.

The experience of living in small towns in Vermont, Alaska and upstate New York – not to mention stays in small villages in Ukraine while volunteering for US AID – had left me with at least a mild understanding of what was taking place. Though it was much friendlier than I'd encountered previously, I was being tested to see if I might fit in. The last thing a small town needs is a nosy interloper or someone flaunting himself about town like he owns the place.

'Yes,' I replied, knowing that they were being polite by mentioning only the bartender as source of their familiarity.

'And we've learned a place to hide the key now, so we won't have to repeat that adventure.'

The stillness of sound, motion and breath that met my response was like that moment of silence in between the screeching of tyres and the sound of impact in a car crash. I didn't know if I was about to slide headlong into a town-shaped brick wall or if my self-effacing manoeuvring had averted the crash. A spectrum of laughter, from high-pitched cackle to deep, coughed croaking, filled the shop and my back was slapped by both the male customers.

I'd apparently passed the test and was tussled to the front of the case as they welcomed me by giving up their places for the American who could make fun of himself. Several minutes of chat surrounded my gathering of rashers, sausages and black and white pudding for our next morning's breakfast. The sausage was 'freshly made by Ford, here' said Mr Sheehy – the distinguished man who I came to learn was the third-generation butcher and owned the shop – as he pointed to the Scot. The black and white pudding prompted a joint dissertation on the best pudding producers in the county, and only the best of the best were represented in the case.

All three butchers – Ford the Scot, Mr Sheehy the owner, and Finbar, the salt-n-pepper haired man – selected, portioned, wrapped and generally assisted me while the rest of the crowd gently interrogated me with questions like, 'What for, here?' as to the reason I was staying in their town in the depths of winter. While the appearance was that the entire assemblage was welcoming me and servicing the new guy as well as possible, I was pretty sure they all wanted to get me wrapped up and out so they could hold a conclave and report to the Town Council. Mr Sheehy made sure that a few extra sausages were tossed into my package after they had been weighed and their price recorded on the package swaddling my rashers. When the total was added and announced, 'Five euro forty', I was greeted with what I would come to know as something of a norm in the smaller shops of The Town.

'Let's make it an even fiver', he said with a nod and placed his finger alongside his nose and winked.

I kid you not! With a gesture I'd only ever read about in books (a 'laying a finger alongside his nose, up the chimney he rose' kind of thing), I was welcomed by a butcher who looked as if he could have been a judge and ushered out the door as if I was a favourite son, home from school. Laugh at yourself and the world laughs with you, I guess … and you may get a discount.

As the part of my brain that hatched the embryonic idea of this winter in the homeland had hoped, the blackthorn walking stick was no longer at the end of the hedgerow when I returned to where I had parked. The 'little people' were indeed at work (or at play), it seemed, and the thought made me both excited and a bit afraid.

11

Breakfast Sundae

A FULL IRISH BREAKFAST is quite something to behold. Producing one on The Cottage's small cooker, with its woeful collection of pots and pans, would have been impossible. While it might sound odd to a reader (and it was a little bit odd for my guests to understand at first as well), I foresaw possible issues in the kitchen and packed a few culinary implements into my extra suitcase.

A cast-iron grill pan, my knives (of course), my favourite loaf tins, one of my prized French clay cooking pots, a bamboo cutting board, coffee and a few 'professional' staples had been tucked in with socks, jumpers and boots. As I choreographed this first meal cooked in the Irish kitchen, something came into razor-sharp focus. If I was going to entertain as many as seven guests at one time, I was going to need to purchase a few more items. For instance, a stock pot that didn't have a crack running from the rim to about halfway down its side and at least one pot with no plastic handles so it could go into the oven. But for this breakfast, I was stuck with what the cupboards provided and the items I had muled across a continent and an ocean. Sadie was still on her schedule from her breeder, who had a farm full of animals, so her days began early. She'd had a much easier time than I with our reveille call before the previous day's drive to Shannon. She let me know she was awake before 5 a.m. by scratching at the door of her Brooks Brothers-lined crate and our day began.

The key firmly in my hand, and the spare key tucked into a secret spot in the hedgerow, we started our day by greeting the sheep. Next came my highly ritualistic relighting of the turf fire in the grate.

I had come to the habit of stoking the fire with a good amount of coal shortly before bedtime. By morning, of course, little was left save small heaps of ash. A few embers, however, could still be found – enough to ignite a bit of kindling or two – and it was my Boy Scout-induced goal to build the morning fire without a single match. On this morning, the crumpled pages of an old phone book I had found when rearranging furniture lit rapidly, and the turf began to catch with hardly any effort.

Next came the brewing of morning coffee and lighting the boiler so the rest of The Cottage could come out of its cold night's slumber. I set the auto-drip to its task and reread the black-faded-to-grey magic marker-written instructions for the heater. All seemed right with the world.

I sat on the wooden floor in front of the boiler with my back against it for the warmth. Sadie came in between my legs for what would become our morning alone time – something we would need with as many guests as were on our calendar. My parents were sleeping off their jet lag and the previous night's post-dinner pub familiarisation. I could have fallen back to sleep as the warm metal behind me took the chill out of my bones. I might have, that is, had it not been for a stream of water that interrupted the morning.

I got to my feet as quickly as I could, and let's just say that my progress wasn't what anyone would call 'quick'. Half of the water I'd poured into the coffee maker was now puddled on the counter top, and gravity had assisted it in dripping down to the floor next to Sadie and me.

I swabbed up the mess from the counter and floor as the final spits and sputters of the pot let me know it was done brewing. Of the ten cups of water I'd placed in the front of the brewing apparatus, only four and a half had completed the process. Now, I like my coffee strong, but shy of half the amount of water meant that I'd effectively doubled the grounds-to-water ratio. I heated fresh water in the electric kettle next to the coffee maker – which I'd used for tea – diluted the coffee syrup, and began digging through the cupboards for an assistive device for our crippled coffee machine.

An old metal tray that was likely used by (and likely nicked by a previous holiday-making tenant from) a local pub served the purpose well.

An aside: though I am jumping several years into another story all together, I must share … When I returned to The Cottage nearly five years later, that same coffee maker sat in the same tray even though I had advised The Princess of the brewer's state of disrepair upon my departure. It was one of many things that hadn't changed about The Cottage upon my return, even though much about me had.

Coffee flood averted and Sadie fed her morning meal, it was now time to turn my attention to the building of our breakfast. The meats I had purchased from the butcher – rashers of Irish bacon, thin breakfast sausages, black and white puddings – were accompanied by broiled tomatoes, baked beans, mushrooms, eggs, fried potatoes and soda bread. Also jam, marmalade, butter, mustard and tangy HP Sauce served as traditional accompaniments to the meal. It was a good thing that my parents' internal clocks were five hours and several pints behind. In my unfamiliar and under-equipped kitchen, breakfast was going to be quite an undertaking. I clicked on the decades-old radio that was part of the kitchen equipment. Rolling the tuning dial from end to end, I was only able to find three stations that came in moderately clear. After I descended and re-ascended the scale to make sure I'd not missed any, I settled on Raidió na Gaeltachta.

For those who have never heard the Irish language, it can sound harsh at first, but if one listens carefully, the lyric qualities of the words reveal themselves. It wouldn't be too far off to think of a marriage between Yiddish and Dutch spoken from the gut, but with a smile. Deep and direct, this ancient language offers occasional extension of warm vowel sounds that keep phrases from sounding too cold. Irish was spoken at least as far back as 300 BC on the island and spread to other Celtic nations over the centuries.

Oven warming, I set to the task of making wheaten bread. This wholemeal variation of soda bread comes from the North of Ireland, and the particular recipe I used was bestowed upon me by the loveliest of innkeepers very near my ancestral town of Lisbellaw, County Fermanagh. She gave me the recipe only if I swore never to share it with anyone. It's the thing my mother covets most, as I've stood fast by my word to keep the recipe secret. The fact that it is called 'wheaten' bread should be your first hint; there's wholemeal flour in this recipe. Whether or not that's the reason I've put it on the menu for her first breakfast in Ireland is conjecture.

Once the bread was baking, I turned my attention to the rest of the tasks at hand. Lovely Kerr's Pink potatoes were scrubbed, peeled and steamed for simple cottage fries, tomatoes halved and topped with seasoned breadcrumbs, and a tin of Batchelors beans was opened and emptied into a small pot to warm. I sliced the 'breakfast mushrooms' (I have no idea, but that's how they were labelled in SuperValu) thick so they could sauté early in the process and hold up in the oven while the rest of breakfast cooked.

I decided to use the hot oven (hint II: the wheaten bread bakes at a rather high temperature) to roast the sausages rather than take up another burner plate on the apartment-sized cooker. Black and white puddings, however, must spend a little time in a hot pan with a bit of fat in order to get the thin, crisp crust I love so. Rashers will also see a hot pan. This may be the only bacon in the world that I'd fry in butter, it being quite lean and from the loin rather than the belly. Rashers benefit from the nutty flavours of the locally churned fat.

At this point in the morning's preparations, I heard Da clomping down the stairs. When he didn't come into the kitchen, I opened the door separating the two main rooms to find him crouching in front of the hot turf, inhaling the hot, mossy fumes.

'I'm really glad you're here,' I said, wanting him to know how special our time together was for me.

He didn't flinch.

Da has lost much of his hearing to nerve damage suffered during his early working life in a soft drink bottling plant for one of the major cola companies. Hearing protection wasn't yet mandated, and it was certainly not manly. Later in life is when we pay for the sins of our youth. Da tried to teach me that lesson with my first car, saying that the bad things you do to an engine, tyres and brakes don't show up at the time of the transgression, but rather they are assessed to the back end of the vehicle's life.

Though my father was also unkind to a number of cars in his youth, I believe he was telling me a story far less automotive than I'd realised at the time.

When he rose and turned toward me, his smile was deep and content. 'Smells like home,' he said, inclining his silver/white-haired head toward the fireplace.

'Coffee's ready,' I said and realised, not for the first time, that I was pantomiming as I spoke so that he'd understand the words he might not hear.

Da settled himself not into a chair at the long kitchen table but rather on the floor next to Sadie's dishes. She gave me the slightest look, as if asking if it was all right, and tumbled to him at my acknowledgment. This really is a smart dog, I thought. The two of them got to know each other and Da pulled an old black comb from his pocket and began to groom her silky locks.

By the time my mother joined us in the now steamy kitchen filled with a gastronomic bouquet of aromas, breakfast was nearly finished. The potatoes had been given their final turn to deepen their crust and colour and the tomatoes had emerged from under the grill. The wheaten bread was sliced, and the pan for eggs nearly preheated. Da had set the table, and together we'd devised a plan to use the kettle and the coffee maker's filter basket as a makeshift pour-through brewing device. A full pot of a famous Seattle coffee now awaited service.

While buffet service would have been the best way to go for our breakfast, I couldn't seem to get the old restaurant ways out of my system. I plated our three meals. Even with very small portions of each of the offerings, the plates looked more like they'd been assembled by a starving man at an all-u-can-eat than by a classically trained chef. By the time I got to the broiled tomatoes, there was no room. So I topped the plates with them as on a meat-laden breakfast sundae.

🌿 🌿 🌿

'I'm not a cooker; I'm an eater,' declared Da as he gathered plates from the table three quarters of an hour later. 'You keep cooking and I'll keep eating. You keep cooking like that and I'll even do the dishes.'

'It's "the washing-up" here, Da,' I remind him, again pantomiming washing a plate.

'All right. You do the cooking up; I'll do the eating up and the "washing-up", then.'

While I'm never comfortable with people I have not paid cleaning up after me in my kitchen (again with the old, professional habits), I learned very early on that people need to be given the opportunity to help. My mother used to answer, 'Just stay out of my way' when a guest would ask if they could help in her kitchen. The look on the faces of friends and family alike taught me early on that taking away someone's ability to help was taking away from some of the shared joy in a completed task.

I excused myself to get ready for a day of exploring. When I ascended the stairs, it was nearly 2.30 p.m. I lay down to put my feet up for a moment or two before showering and fell into a deep, MS-induced sleep. It's the kind of sleep that is like anaesthesia; you don't know how long you've been out, you wake in the same exact position you fell away, and you don't feel particularly rested.

A note, in Da's sweeping, left-handed handwriting greeted me on the table:

> Took Sadie-Pup to explore The Town. Your mother made some bacon sandwiches on your bread; they're in the fridge. We'll meet you at The Bridge for a pint at 6.
>
> – Da

I thought about the Mother scouring the cupboards looking for the bread recipe as she made the sandwiches, not realising I kept it hidden in the bag of flour.

Raidió na Gaeltachta was still on the small radio and I noted that it was nearly 6 p.m. already. I sat and ate my sandwich to the faint soundtrack of uillean pipes and bodhrán, staring out the window at the ewes grazing on sweet grasses. Full Irish Breakfasts, I decided, would only be prepared once per week. I'd dreamed of this time for decades and I could not – would not – lose hours of it each day recovering from equal hours spent in the kitchen. It was a good lesson to learn so early on in the trip, and my parents were good guests with whom to learn it.

Another lesson: Mr Sheehy's dry-cured rashers made the BEST bacon sandwiches, EVER.

12

Reunion

I BELIEVE IT COULD BE said that my parents were equally looking forward to their entire stay in The Town, up to this point, as they were to the last few days of their visit when my house guests overlapped. Sheri, my former wife, and a dear friend of ours, Bridgett, were slated for arrival four days prior to my parents' flight out of Dublin.

The people who know and love us can totally understand why Sheri and I are still so close after our divorce. Those who don't get it either do not know us and our history or are no longer in our lives. For readers who cannot possibly know the history that the two of us share, I simply ask that you suspend your disbelief for the sake of this tale. Just know there is still respect and true love in our relationship even though we are no longer married. That said, yes, the woman to whom I was married for nearly seventeen years – and from whom I had been separated for over five years and divorced for three – was coming to visit me in Ireland, and my parents were ecstatic to see her.

It had been about six years since Sheri and my parents had last seen one another. Cards and calls were regularly exchanged, but even though I lived only 80 miles from Sheri, and Da had visited me a couple of times since our separation, they hadn't had the opportunity to spend time together. It was too bad, really. Like true old friends, though, we all knew we were in for half a week of craic.

I could tell the 'rents were excited by the way they went about helping me prepare the sleeping closet for the impending arrival. The chest of drawers was dragged around to block a cupboard door. The cupboard was only big enough to store the new linens and towels I'd purchased for the guest room, so blocking its door didn't do any harm and freed up enough space that the bunk beds could be un-stacked. Can you see a woman, nearly fifty, climbing into the top bunk … after a session down the pub?

Though there would be room enough to sidle between the freshly un-bunked beds, making them up was impossible. The beds were re-stacked, made up, and then re-un-bunked with fresh sheets, cases and quilted blankets. Considering the age of both mattresses and pillows, I was pretty sure the sheets, cases, and quilts would be the softest and most cushioning of the entire ensemble. From my experience with my bedroom's furnishings, I could say so with some authority. Though the incoming flight was scheduled to arrive around midday, the 'rents were not joining me for the pick-up. There was no way that we would all five (plus Sadie) fit into the skate-ball bag. Remembering how Sheri used to pack made me wonder if I, the two ladies, and the fruits of their over-packing were going to fit. Even Sadie's small displacement was suspect, so I set off for Shannon alone on the brightest sunny day we'd had since my arrival.

Sheri and Bridgett had flown from Seattle to Shannon via Copenhagen, Denmark. They had, therefore, been in an airport or on a plane for nearly twenty hours. You wouldn't have known it. They both looked good; Sheri always looked good. But I could tell that it was still the middle of the night for their bodies. As the sun was well over the yardarm, and they needed nourishment, I decided that a quick pub stop for lunch on our way home would be called for.

One thing just about every pub in Ireland can be counted upon to deliver, along with a good pint, of course, is soup and a decent toasted sandwich.

Often the soup is vegetable soup and if it is, it's far more common that what arrives in your bowl looks more like an infant's pap than soup. Don't get me wrong; these soups can be incredibly complex and nuanced in flavour. Yet no matter the flavour, I just can't get past the texture of a soup that can fully support a spoon in standing position. I therefore opt for the de facto national dish: the ham and cheese toastie with onion and tomato.

I said that 'just about every pub in Ireland can be counted on' for a decent toasted sandwich. On this day, with sun shining bright and two beautiful women travellers on their first trip to Ireland, I found one of the very few that cannot.

While I found the establishment suspect from the moment we walked in the front door, I knew when we spotted it that we would soon be out of options, at least for several miles. That the place was all but empty at the tail end of the luncheon hours should, possibly, have been an indicator. However, it would be nearly an hour before we were in the vicinity of another. By that time lunch service would be over. The time, coupled with Sheri's forecastable descent of attitude when her blood sugar got too low, made this our only serviceable choice for a lunch stop.

The soup – vegetable, as I could have divined – was at least not the expected slurry. Rather, it was condensed beef/vegetable, straight from the tin. The publican was also serving as the lunch shift cook. It would not surprise me to hear that he had run to the supermarket and fetched the tin off the shelf moments after we inquired after the day's soup selection. Our toasties arrived at table still in the miniature equivalent of the 'brown-in-the-bag' turkey roasting plastic my mother once tried for a Thanksgiving dinner with limited success. Okay, like most of her turkeys, with no real success.

While this first Irish lunch together would not be considered a culinary success, we were at least sated and warmed, the 'warmed' bit of particular import as we stepped from the pub into a stiffening breeze which foretold a change in weather.

🖋 🖋 🖋

The welcome that met us at The Cottage was warm in many ways. Da had loaded enough turf into the fireplace that you'd have thought he was expecting our arrival from the Arctic. The hug shared by Da and Sheri was warm enough to make someone who didn't know them or the situation less than comfortable. Sheri is nine years my senior and I was born when my father was only eighteen.

It was often the joke when the two of them were together that, were my mother to kick the bucket and I to do something stupid, they'd probably have enjoyed dating. It's not really as icky as it sounds now that I read what I have just written. If you knew us, you'd see the humour in it. Since you don't know us, I'll simply have to once again ask your disbelief to be suspended. It's just what works for Sheri and me.

I too was greeted warmly – more warmly than I'd imagined I would be. Sadie bound out the Dutch door when it was opened as the skate-ball bag slid to rest. She leapt into my lap while I was still in the driver's seat and buckled in. By the time I could unfasten my seat belt and hoist her to the ground, my ears, face, and any hair that extended from under my cap were fully anointed by what would henceforth be known as 'Sadie Kisses'. While she was interested in the newest additions to our household, she paid them only socially required notice and figure-of-eighted my legs all the way inside The Cottage. She stopped only long enough to stamp at the sheep who had gathered to welcome us. Much to her satisfaction, they scattered en masse.

I was surprised at the depth of her loyalty to her new pack leader. We'd been together for only eleven days and now we'd added two more faces to what she must have begun to see as her new pack. For all the assaults to her canine sensibilities, Sadie was seeing me, or at least treating me, as the constant and her alpha. Just before we stepped out of the coming storm and into the peat-scented dry sauna that was now The Cottage, Sadie stopped and turned to the one sheep that did not scurry and gave her a good stamp with her front paws. When the ewe only flinched, Sadie wiggled herself in place and stamped paws yet again. Once more, with feeling.

The sheep ran and Herself turned and looked at me with pride, as if to say, 'I've got the sheep under control, Da. You're the Alpha dog, but I'm the Alpha bitch.'

I bent to pick her up and carry her into the house and was rolled right onto my back by the force of her advance. Rather than sit and look at me – turtled as I was – like the day we hiked for our spare key, she jumped onto my chest and showered me with more Sadie Kisses.

Miller's restaurant was quickly becoming everyone's first dinner upon arrival. By evening, as we left the place, the wind that had begun to freshen after our dismal lunch had become what the locals call 'desperate', and it finally ushered in the winter rain my Seattle friends had foretold. Though they had all spurned my offer to take any of them along with me when I decided to strap on the skate-ball bag for the descent into town, my lodgers all required my chauffeuring services to return them to our near-capacity abode.

Even without Sadie and luggage, there was no shoe-horning our entire party into our miniature conveyance. Da offered to be in the first sortie and stoke the fire with the new sack of hard Czech coal we'd purchased at a filling station the next village over. My mother joined him, and while there may – may – have been room for one more, Sheri and Bridgett agreed to tuck themselves into a nearby pub for one. I'd gather them after getting the auld ones in for the night.

Knowing how one thing leads to another or, as Da put it that night, 'Slap leads to tickle,' I was sent away from The Cottage with explicit instructions to take the girls out for a proper night on the Irish town.

'Besides,' said he, 'you've already become The Town scandal by walking around in your PJs. Why not show off with two beautiful women on your arms?'

Never one to disobey my father, especially when he was all but commanding me to get these two hotties all liquored up, I put on my drinking shoes and dismounted the hill for a few pints and a few laughs. If nothing else, Sheri and I could still laugh, and Bridgett made her comic intentions known to me the very first time we were introduced at the wedding reception.

'You'd better treat her right, you, you … You Young Buck Penis!' she'd said. It took me not a short while to unravel threat from humour – two years in fact. Not until she came to visit Sheri and me at our first home together in Swampscott, Massachusetts did I finally cement her behaviour to be on the side of clownishness.

Shedding cap, coat and muffler soaked by the increasing rain in just the short distance between the car park and the public house, I found the girls at a low table about halfway down the room from the bar and the stage. A hot whiskey ornamented the place in front of each of them, while a dark pint of stout and a golden dram of something higher on the proof scale stood at attention for my arrival. The music had not yet begun, it being only 9.30 p.m. The musicians were scheduled for 9 p.m., but punctuality is seen as an affliction within the musical set. The place was already better than two thirds full and brimming with happy sounds.

I sat and picked up the pint in one sweeping motion and raised it to toast my fellow conspirators.

'Bridgett wants to know if we're going to have sex,' blurted Sheri before Your One could playfully slap her for asking.

'All three of us?' I asked. 'The beds don't seem that strong, do you think?' I added, before taking three long swallows from my pint.

By the time my glass was returned to its mat, we were enveloped in the joyous, nasty laughter that we three had shared in our younger days.

'You're all yak and no shack, Sheri,' I said, and we laughed and drank and laughed and sang along with the players, who had finally arrived somewhere after the giggling began but before the cackling.

Knowing that it was far too desperate out to walk, even if my legs would have afforded me the opportunity, I kept myself to one pint and let the girls share my 'cold' whiskey as they sipped their second hot. We prepared ourselves for the weather I had come in from, but the storm had taken advantage of the time to build to a North Atlantic blow that would had made the Bering Sea proud. Even if I had kept up with the girls drink for drink, I would have been sobered by the rain, which seemed to have no particular direction of origin. Each drop's destination seemed targeted at we three and our skate-ball bag transport.

When we turned off the laneway into the drive, we were greeted by a colour about which I'd only ever read. Da had, indeed, turned that bag of rock dug from well beneath Eastern Europe into heat – and various greenhouse gases. The glow that emanated from the living room window – past, through and around the cotton-laced curtains – was a red-orange the likes of which we conjure in our brains when we think of sweating men, stripped to their waists, feeding industrial furnaces or locomotives by the shovelful. Particles of dust in the air inside the room seemed illuminated by an energy emitting from the hearth while the drops of rain outside the window were turned to molten glass as they passed through its radiant beam.

I cut the headlights and coasted in by the warm summons of this beacon.

Looking in the window from the storm, I saw the tired old furniture and fixtures The Princess had cobbled together transformed into a drawing room from times gone by. Faded patterns leapt from worn tapestry and shadows cast lamps as statuary and framed prints as masterworks of another day. And there on her fleece, stretched out on her belly and looking aflame as a Navaho sunset, was my dear Sadie. She had positioned herself close enough to the blaze for warmth without being so close as to overheat. She looked closer than would be comfortable for me, even if heat and MS didn't mix like a scarecrow and a lit match.

She lay on her belly with her back legs spread out and one front bent backward, looking like a seal pup that had injured its front flipper. A bright orange seal pup. I almost didn't want to open the door to disturb the slumbering roan, but the drops of rain were beginning to feel as searing as they looked and the wind was finding every seam in my coat.

13

All Creatures

BY THE TIME SADIE's bladder brought us both down the stairs the next morning, the rain had let up a bit, but the storm seemed far from blowing itself into its final act. I reached the bottom of the stairs, a position that leaves one next to and perpendicular to the fireplace. That's when reality grabbed hold of my tired brain and its flood-control-trained part awakened.

Not only had the fire gone out, it looked as if it had been put out by an overambitious boy scout with too much water on hand. The muddy slurry of the ash of coal and turf was studded with a few clinkers and beginning to swirl beneath the grate. Our chimney was transformed into a black waterfall as thin streams of water trickled from stone to wetted stone, feeding the growing ash lake.

I grabbed the bucket and the new scoop I'd purchased that first morning to replace the plastic dustpan The Princess had provided for removing ash. A bit of creative sculpting and I'd formed a dam of wet ash and newspaper wadded up from the kindling basket. Only then was I able to begin transferring scoopfuls of thick, dark grey water from fireplace to bucket. It was a slow process. I was far more adept at using the scoop to remove dry ash than I was at using it as a ladle for this soup.

Sadie seemed to take great interest in the process, getting herself very nearly covered in the slop on more than one transfer. I couldn't scold her for her curiosity. Had I been a young boy of her equivalent age in dog years, I would have been enthralled as well. (At this point, I figured she was nearly six and in full childhood discovery mode.) I was just happy that she was paying attention to the action rather than following nature's morning call.

And then, as if reading my mind, she turned her bum to the grate, squatted and peed. I covered her puddle with a fresh wad of newsprint so as not to interrupt my current process. Sadie dismounted the hearth, strode to her fleece, and lay down to watch the rest of whatever it was that her Da was doing until he got around to feeding her breakfast.

Kids and dogs: you just can't work with them.

Whether it was a change in diet or the stress of her new home and all of these people in it, Sadie's nervous digestive system warranted a trip to the local veterinarian. It was about time I visited the vet as well.

Upon learning of my plans to winter in Kerry, my MS specialist had shown great concern for my health. Along with his impressive team, he is known around the world for his impassioned clinical treatment of multiple sclerosis and scientific research.

'The words "Ireland" and "Neurologist" don't find their way into the same sentence very often, Trevis,' he'd told me with a wry smile.

That I wasn't going to be staying in, or even near, a major city was of concern to him as well. While I had been getting progressively 'better' since I started the chemotherapy treatments nearly three years earlier, I had completed my last allowable lifetime dosing just a month before leaving America. The disease had gotten virulent during my first eighteen months after diagnosis. We switched to the nuclear option of the day from my original therapy, which had been the first approved drug for the treatment of MS only a few years before I was diagnosed.

'If your MS is getting this aggressive, Trevis,' my doctor advised, 'we should get aggressive right back.'

The treatments weren't a cakewalk, let me assure you of that. I'll not, however, say that they were as bad as I had anticipated. Every three months I would simply take myself out of circulation – or any social contact, really – while my immune cells were bombed all the way back to the bone marrow.

Every quarter I would check myself into the university hospital and roll up my sleeve for a dose of 'The Blue Juice'. The drug was a most beautiful shade of deep, federal blue. The colour, I was later to learn, had actually been developed as a carpet dye for the United States Bicentennial in 1976. I've often wondered, throughout my life, from where this idea or that product might have germinated. In the case of my MS treatment, it had come from making sure that the Blue in our 200-year-old Red, White and Blue was vibrant enough for the occasion.

When the nurses came to infuse me with the deeper-than-royal liquid, they cloaked themselves in special gowns, double gloves with latex thicker than most dishwashing hand wear and donned not only protective goggles, but also clear full-face shields. Nothing says 'Show us your veins' like a medical professional with a bag of carpet dye, a needle and full hazmat gear.

For two or three days after treatment I would pee the most amazing shades of green as my kidneys filtered out the pigments of my patriotic medication. After that, I would become more and more anaemic and weak as the chemicals stayed toxic in my system for about ten days. During that time I would imagine my blood was some kind of poisonous environment for my poor, misguided immune cells – the ones that found the protective sheath around my nerves an irresistible snack. By day twelve or thirteen after treatment, I was at my lowest energy level and most susceptible to infection.

Predictably, though, waking on day fourteen would be a full Williamson turn from the course I'd been on when I retired the previous night. (That's a manoeuvre I learned in the Coast Guard which is used to bring a ship back to a point previously passed through but in the opposite direction.) It was as if my brain was aware of my body's lack of immune protection and had sent signals to my bone marrow to boost production – thus the increased weakness, as more and more energy was used to create the cannon fodder that were my T-cells in this exercise. Once my blood was no longer a hostile environment, my body was fully repopulated with defence warriors and my energy levels returned to near normal.

Now that I was done with my high-on-the-colour-spectrum infusions, however, my doc was worried that I might slip into my previous pattern of attacks. Not one to go into situations without having a few of those 'what ifs' answered, I asked about options. Corticosteroid infusions every day for three to five days were really the only thing that could be done when the disease decides to advance and take more of what it seemed hungry for, meaning me.

'From what I read in your chart and what our nurse practitioner tells me, it would have to get pretty bad before you'd opt for steroids again,' said the doc during my pre-departure visit, 'but that's really all there is to offer.'

'Well,' I told him, 'The Town does have a GP, but no hospital within a forty-five-minute drive. There is a really good vet.' I knew. I'd been checking after my potential puppy's medical well-being.

When I tell you that I chose my MS doc for his international renown, his clinical prowess and his personality that, like mine, tends a little toward the geeky, I am not being wholly forthcoming. This guy has a sense of humour and by the look on his face he was seeing the picture as I was painting it.

'Large animal or small?' he asked.

'Both; companion and farm,' I replied, unsure exactly where he was going with this but willing to give him more line.

'Well, he'd have the drugs and he'd have needles about the right size,' he pondered. 'I'll write a letter of introduction along with a prescription, just in case. Thirty years in medicine and this is the first time I've written an order to be fulfilled by a country veterinarian ... in another country. It feels very *All Creatures Great and Small* to me.'

And that was that – settled. If his colleagues read this book, they'll know the doctor of whom I write and each will smile knowingly.

So, off Sadie and I went to meet her new doctor, get something for her tummy, and introduce myself as his potential new patient; quite possibly, but not definitely, his first with only two legs. Even if they are not two *good* legs.

✦ ✦ ✦

The vet, as it turns out, *was* very *All Creatures Great and Small*. While waiting to have Sadie seen, I chatted up the other pet owners whose dogs and bitches were awaiting their turn in the surgery. We touched on subjects ranging from pet food to places I might let Herself off-lead for a good romp. All the animals waiting to be seen were pets or companion animals. The working dogs would be tended to when the veterinary was on his rounds to farms – rounds he made every day, Sundays included if need be.

One topic I asked about that no one seemed to be able to answer had to do with boarding. We had a trip to Dublin planned to see Da and Mother off to the airport and I had a surprise overnight planned for Sheri and Bridgett after the 'rents departed. Sadie could neither ride the train with us to Dublin nor would she be welcomed on the second trip. I needed a place to look after Herself and I was hoping to be rather particular about where that might be.

The veterinary concluded that I might be feeding Sadie a bit too much, and therein lay her 'issues'. A cursory check of my veins also ensured that he did, indeed, have needles and catheters of proper size, were they needed. Finally I asked if he knew of any boarding facilities not too far out of the way of our travel plans. As it happened, he had a card from a place that had just opened. He'd boarded his wife's dog there just a few weeks earlier while they took advantage of the October bank holiday to travel to London to see his sister's new baby.

Say what you will about small towns being closed societies. He opened his wallet and pulled out the receipt for the stay to give me the phone numbers and showed me the prices and everything. In one short visit he not only saw to Sadie's medical needs and my potential and theoretical ones, he also told me about his sister's baby, the 'ruddy Brit' she'd married (his words, not mine), and much about his wife's pet, which was recorded on the invoice. Maybe a pyjamaed excursion was, in fact, a very good way to introduce oneself to a new town.

The next afternoon everyone else in the house intended to make a day of shopping in The Town. I took advantage of their absence to arrange a visit to the kennels.

Making telephone calls from a phone box in a country town is not the easiest task if one doesn't know some background information. Not knowing which calling area I was in made it a bit difficult. Enter too many numbers and the call wouldn't go through. Dial too few, and again, no call. Each time, however, I was still charged for the call or for the non-call in these cases. Finally reaching the receiver of my intended call, I was given instructions to the kennels just outside of The Other Larger Town. Like many driving directions given by people who know the area, these were nuanced with local landmarks and characters. Some of my favourites tell you what's in the direction of each exit from a roundabout before the exit you really want. 'You'll come into the roundabout at the bottom – six o'clock, like – and go past the first road out. That would take you down past the Auld Triangle, which is a fine pub if you wanted to hear some of the local music. Now, the second road you'd take if you wanted to head up county, but you don't want that one. You could take the third road off but that would take you through town before you got here and it would be a lot more turns for ye … unless, of course, you wanted to do some shopping on your way. Do you want to do any shopping on your way?' That's how you might hear it told.

Another type of Irish direction-giving is indicating where to turn off the main road by telling you what you might not know … yet.

'Oh, I'd say it's about four or so miles before ye'd have to turn off that road. It'll be the hard left about two hundred yards before you get to the burial ground. You won't see the burial ground. It's around a couple of bends after the turn. If you've come to the burial ground, cross yourself and drive past, up to O'Connor's Hardware. You can turn around there and head back the way ye came. But then, of course, it'd be a right turn, not a left and it'd be after the couple of bends that will be past the burial ground. You know which burial ground I'm tellin' you about, right?'

Wendy was the name of the boarder. From then on I'd refer to her as 'The Wendy Lady' to Sadie. Taken from the film *Hook*, the name had a sound I liked, and Herself liked it too. Opening my Ordnance Survey map – which had cost me nearly €8 – and unfolding the piece of paper on which I'd scrawled Wendy's instructions, I was able to put some order and a visual representation to the 'left ats' and 'don't go pasts'. I wasn't sure I'd be able to make the trip without a local gazetteer for all the specifics I was recited, but it was worth packing a compass and my trusty sextant for our voyage of introduction.

Worst case scenario: I'd stop at a pub and ask for assistance. One can't just barge into an establishment and demand orientation to the local nomenclature. These things must be done with tact and finesse … and ordering a pint doesn't hurt either.

14

Cloud of White

WITH SADIE'S LODGING arranged, we were next set to conceive our joint conveyance and transfer to the train station in The Other Larger Town. I was happy to know that my time with the skate-ball bag was nearing its end, for I'd arranged to swap vehicles when I deposited Sheri and Bridgett at Shannon. That didn't help the fact that we were now five people, with three of us packing overnight bags and the 'rents going home laden with one more suitcase than they'd arrived with.

The Town had prospered from their stay, thanks to Mother's love of many things Irish and Da's willingness to sit in a pub and soak up the atmosphere, chat up the occasional loud-speaking publican, and generally make himself scarce while Mother enriched the local coffers.

A taxi could have been arranged, but it was a 45-minute drive. Most people in Kerry didn't travel that way, so Your Man would have to come back without a fare and was likely to charge us for that time as well. Bus Éireann was an option, particularly because the bus depot shared space with the train station in The Other Larger Town. Schedules, however, made this choice less than optimal.

The final option, outside of the course eventually elected, was to ask a lift of a local who might be going that way. Hitching a ride in Ireland isn't frowned upon like it is in America, and it wasn't all that long ago that an automobile wasn't something most families had. Surely a couple of forlorn septuagenarians alongside the roadway with extended thumbs would quickly get a lift. I thought it best, however, not to even present the idea as an option to the group.

The only choice that held any water whatsoever was still less than optimal. I would drive two shifts of passengers the three-quarter hour one-way trip to the train depot. That would make for two and a quarter hours of drive time. Figuring in transfers at the station, reloading and a cushion of a few minutes before the train departed, a three-hour head start on the departure schedule seemed ample … then.

I clocked the trips just to make sure, in real time, the night prior to our adventure when I took Herself to the Wendy Lady's for boarding. Though the kennel wasn't very far from the train station, the added stress of the additional trip and having to say goodbye to my puppy for the first time were more than I was willing to heap onto an already high-pressure endeavour. Let's remember, I was ferrying my parents and my ex-wife here …

I even thought myself quite clever when I was able to load ALL of the luggage and souvenir bags into the skate-ball bag for the first leg with Sheri and Bridgett. This would cut off the chunk of time I'd allotted for loading bags in between trips.

Leg one went as smoothly as could be expected. I may have heavy-footed the drive a bit for all the weight currently balanced above the axles. Sheri, in fact, let out the occasional 'HEYyyyyy!' in response to the testing I was giving the shock absorbers. She tried, on a couple of occasions, to correct my driving pattern. I simply replied to her nagging with, 'You don't get to do that any more …' We three have gotten years of laughter from, and considerable reuse of, that line. I deposited Load One near the station, so they could spend the next ninety minutes or so poking around the shops of The Other Larger Town, which we'd not yet even had time to explore. Then I was off on my return voyage. My eager accelerator foot had even picked me up a few minutes. I used the moments to stop at a filling station deli to order sandwiches for the trip, which I would pick up as I passed with my final load of human cargo. Two ham and butter, two turkey and cheddar, and two rasher sandwiches, all on brown bread and cut in half, I figured, would offer more than enough selection for our far from persnickety appetites.

Even with my stop, I was ahead of schedule when I broke toward the mountain road at the fork that goes left to the shore road and right to the mountain. As I wound along the portion of the mountain road that follows a small brook, however, all of that changed.

Past bucolic farms and cottages, I wove the skate-ball bag through the countryside as if I were driving the latest model Jaguar – in touring green, of course, for a television advertisement. Working the gears like I was driving in the Le Mans Classic, I grew accustomed to the ticking of hedges on mirror, which had become a soft percussive soundtrack. I'll not deny a few Vroom Vrooms may have escaped me. Then it all kind of stopped.

Rounding the last curve before a longish straight stretch, I saw something that I was sure they only staged for tourist films and the occasional shearing festival. A cloud of white had descended the hillside and taken up its course opposite mine. Beside and behind the cloud, three men walked along and twice that number of Border collies patrolled. A flock was being moved from one place to the next and I, along with my no-longer-a-Jag, was now on a tarmacked version of a pasture-to-pasture trail.

With hardly enough road for two cars to pass, there was no moving over to the shoulder. As it was, I was using the now-bare fuchsia like Buddy Rich used brushes on his snare. Nothing could be done for space or for time but to take skate-ball bag out of gear, turn on my hazards, and wait to be enveloped by the bleating cloud of wool and hooves that showed every intention of perambulating around me on all sides.

I could see past the herd, where there was a short line of four or five cars following at parade pace. My guess is that it wasn't unlike driving behind horses in a parade, when it came to dodging the landmines they were known to drop in the road. I could only surmise that this was either a) commonplace for the drivers, if they were locals or b) quite the memorable experience if they were tourists.

A few of them must have been on tour, for I could also see cameras sticking out a few windows. I was expecting my experience to be a bit more thrilling as I was to be overtaken by the beasts. I had no idea, however, how thrilling and potentially expensive my half of the encounter would prove.

Smiles of the passing herders were replaced by shock on the face of Your Man at the back of the bunch. After about one third of the flock passed by a parting of the White Sea, one of the lazy buggers decided that going around the obstacle to progress that I had become was a waste of his time and/or energy. Up onto the bonnet of the car jumped the sheep who couldn't be bothered to go around. Countless of his fellow pilgrims followed suit. In due course the dogs decided that their charges shouldn't be taking the skate-ball bag as a ramp. Three of them mounted the car to escort those already in transit off the bonnet, roof and boot. One stayed on the bonnet to deter others as his comrades retook chase of their woolly wards.

Stunned beyond words and well into my ability to form a thought beyond 'I wish Sadie had been here,' I rolled down my window to greet the man ushering the last of the ewes past. 'Jea-sus, I'm sorry!' said Your Man. 'Is it a hired car?' as if anyone in their right mind would buy a car of such poor breeding.

'Aye,' I fumbled out. 'Does that happen often?' I was still gob-smacked by the episode.

'No, not usually with the ewes,' he replied. He stopped and leaned in my window, smelling very much of musky lanolin from that lack of distance. 'But there are a few young rams me Da is moving to market. Are ya stayin' near here? We'll buff those marks and Dan Dooley'll never know what happened.' That was the name of the omnipresent Irish rental car agency that I had not used.

'I'm staying in The Town for the winter and don't have to return the car for about a week,' I said, finally finding my words.

'That's our house back there,' he said, pointing to the last farmhouse I'd passed. 'Bring her by and we'll clean it up for you.'

'I'm actually going to take the train to Dublin from The Other Larger Town today and won't be back until Tuesday. Would Tuesday work?'

'Are ya leaving her in the car park at the station?' he asked and I affirmed.

'I'm going up there tomorrow. I'll bring my brother along and you'll never know it happened when you see her,' he promised.

'Really?!' I couldn't come up with anything better than that. Sorry to say, but as much as I'd like to report that my time that far into the stay had afforded me access to a retort matching the extraordinary nature of the situation, 'Really?!' was all I could muster.

'Good as done,' says he and then he was off to catch up with the others.

Honks, waves and a few good-natured thumbs-ups came from the cars that ended the Ovis-ian cavalcade. What an amazing story to tell … to people. Like those who were waiting for me to transfer them to the train station.

After going up the mountain and most of the way down, I refilled with passengers and once again ascended the mountain road from the side of The Cottage. At the sight of Da's inquiring face, I promised to explain the obviously altered condition of the vehicle. Back down the other side, we passed the place of the happening and then came upon the farm that was the flock's destination.

Behind a now-closed gate, my mother noted aloud that there seemed to be an 'awful lot of sheep in that yard. And look at the dogs, too. Do you think they're going to move them down the road? Wouldn't that be fun to see?' Yes, Mother. It was pretty fun to see.

All of my spare time had been squandered along with a substantial chunk that I did not have to spare. The pre-packing of my parents' bags came in handy, as did the pre-ordering of the sandwiches. Not having the time to be bothered with change, I left the lass who handed me my sandwiches to pocket what could be considered a pretty fair tip. I took the bag of goods, dropped two €20 notes on the counter, and looked at her to see if it would do.

An astonished nod came from her as I bolted for the door and the still-running and quite-marred car.

We made the train with just a bit of time to spare, and everyone boarded without incident. I unpacked our meal as I regaled my companions with the story of the stampede. When I finished, I noted that no one had touched their food. I thought it due to my riveting retelling of the events. In actuality, Mother and Da had eaten something from the fridge in The Cottage while Sheri and Bridgett availed themselves of a local café during my harrowing absence.

They were the worst €40 sandwiches I'd ever tasted.

15

Drinking the President's Whiskey

UPON OUR RETURN rail voyage from Dublin, I was happy but more than a bit surprised to see that our skate-ball bag had indeed been buffed and washed. Were I to be honest, it looked better than when I'd picked it up nearly three weeks before. Only a couple of small dents in the roof were evident, and the herding lads had even buffed out the traces of my near-constant hedgerow encounters.

I pretty much remembered the way to the Wendy Lady's kennels, only missing one turn and not having to drive too far in order to find a place to reverse course. While the sun was still well above the horizon, we found our way to her gate. Sheri and Bridgett stayed in the car while I got out to collect Herself. They'd obviously not had enough in the way of business interaction with the folks in Kerry. Wendy wasn't particularly chatty by Irish standards, but relative to most transactions in the USA we were at it for a good while.

I learned much about Wendy's establishment as we gathered Sadie's bed, toys, food, bowls and suitcase. I kid about the suitcase, but the way I'd packed for her, you'd have thought she was a real little girl on her first sleepover.

The building Wendy used for boarding was purpose-built and very new. She'd only opened her business that autumn and already she was considering expanding.

'So,' said I as we watched Sadie roughhouse with some of her new-found pals in a large double-fenced play area, 'that's not a Kerry accent you've got there.'

'And neither is yours,' she responded.

I guessed I was 'doing' it again with the accent. I explained, with a bit of embarrassment. She was surprised that I was not actually from Ireland, and I'll admit my surprise to find out where she was from as well.

'Just north of Boston,' she replied to the natural inquiry that followed.

'Oh,' said I, 'I used to live in Swampscott' (pronounced Sw'amp-skit if you're from there) 'on the naath shaa,' to emphasise that I'd live there long enough to speak in the vernacular. Her countenance altered when I said 'Swampscott,' and I thought I was going to have to repeat the town's name in a less colloquial fashion.

'Swampskit?!' she said, startled. 'My mother's from Swampskit!'

Hand to God, her mother lived on my street, a few houses away and on the other side, but I could see her house from mine. Though I didn't know her mother, I knew the house and I remembered her from the walks Sheri and I would take around the neighbourhood. Another of those little things that seem to happen in Ireland.

Wendy had moved her mother with her to The Other Larger Town about ten years earlier and her mum was now in nursing care. I asked to be remembered to her, even if we'd only ever said 'hello' once or twice. Here I was, 5,000 miles from my current hometown, nearly 3,000 from the first place Sheri and I lived as a married couple, and I was boarding my new dog with the daughter of an old neighbour. Only in Ireland.

My passengers seemed a bit annoyed at the time it had taken to simply pick up a dog, but I was excited to explain. Maybe it was because we were all tired from the day's travels, maybe because the skate-ball bag was cramped, even with all of our overnight bags fitting into the boot. Maybe I'll never know for sure, but my thought is that the sweet memories of our newly-wed time in that quaint seaside town, layered with the spicy romance of Kerry, and iced with the bitter frosting that is lost potential made for a layer cake of emotions that made the story a difficult dessert for Sheri to swallow.

Seventeen years of marriage to the woman taught me to know when not to press, and we shifted the conversation to our next adventure: an honest-to-goodness castle.

✎ ✎ ✎

Just a few days later we four were under way again with Sadie in tow. For this trip I'd made arrangements for her to stay with the resident gamekeeper. We entered the grounds of Dromoland Castle in County Clare to the strains of Christy Moore's 'Ride On'. I was happy to see the old buildings and meticulously tended grounds again. Stately yet welcoming, the staff of this regal property had treated me and all of my guests like family during my previous visits.

Sheri and Bridgett were struck dumb by the majesty of the scene as we entered the main gates and wound about through manicured fairways and greens. An audible gasp escaped them in tired unison when the castle revealed itself to us as the drive gently curved between forest and lake. Their sighs masked my own.

The drive of over four hours, after weeks of chauffeuring first my parents and then this duo around the sights of The Town and its environs in the cramped quarters of the manual-transmissioned skate-ball bag had taken their toll on my body. My left leg and arm, most affected by MS, had been wrecked by the constant working of clutch and wheel as I upshifted and downshifted round loping curves and hairpin turns. Not to mention the toll it took to slow behind tractors and other vehicles of questionable road-worthiness and then race to pass the same before oncoming traffic or topography took away the leapfrog opportunity.

The castle was an even more welcome sight when the bell staff greeted all of us warmly, then me by name. They hefted our bags and supported me up the stairs to the entry foyer.

Were it not authentic, the lobby of the castle might be considered a bit kitschy. This is what marks the difference between a Disneyfied replica and the real article: the suits of armour are real, the hand-hued stone is a bit stained from four centuries of service, and the guest register is signed by presidents and heads of state from scores of nations. Perhaps the carpets are a bit threadbare here and there and some of the décor has fallen out of fashion and returned again at least three times. The castle offers tangible comfort and constants such as the warm handshake and heartfelt 'Ye are very welcomed' with which we were greeted at the reception desk.

Also awaiting us, freshly summonsed from the bar where he and his staff of loaders and beaters were drinking pints bought by the appreciative gunmen, was the felt- and tweed-clad keeper of the castle's game – pheasant, ducks, trout and a large herd of stag. He greeted Sadie by name and scooped her into his sturdy arms and was lavishly rewarded with wet kisses, which he relished. I knew for certain that Sadie was, quite literally at this point, in good hands for her part of our stay.

Refreshed from the day's shoot, he took Herself off to meet the hounds that serviced the organised hunts held on the estate. These hunts furnish the kitchen's adept staff with wonderful game for the evening table. Today, however, was our American Thanksgiving, and we would be supping on a specially arranged 'traditional' dinner. On any other day, I would be salivating over the thought of Chef's preparation of the day's kill.

🍂 🍂 🍂

I came down for dinner, fresh from a well-earned and rather lengthy kip and an amazing, and quite lengthy, soak under a dinner-plate-sized showerhead. My glass of sherry had just arrived at my table alongside the bar's roaring fireplace when the girls arrived. They had spent the afternoon touring the walled garden and pampering themselves with a pedicure at the castle's spa. We warmed our livers with spirits, our bodies by the fire, and our appetites with an afore gaze at the evening's menu.

Six full courses were to be offered, including the first time I'd ever read of a 'pre-dessert' course on a menu. The turkey was to be served in the Irish style. 'Turkey-Ham' or 'Turkey-Bacon' can be found on many a public house menu in the country. That Chef would offer his version of the creation was exciting to me beyond compare.

I explained to my dinner companions that a generous mound of stuffing, made from day-old soda bread, onion, herbs and the like, is topped with slices of Irish bacon or cured/smoked ham and then roast turkey breast. The whole is then napped with a creamy and nutmeg-laced béchamel flecked with a generous handful of dark green, chopped parsley.

Though she didn't remember the fact, I had made my first béchamel – the 'mother' white sauce of classical, French cooking – for Sheri long before I was trained as a chef. She came to visit me at my home in Kodiak, Alaska, when we were engaged, and it topped our potatoes at brunch like a warm, woollen blanket on a cold, February day. It is a sauce as easy to make as it is to screw up, as simple as it is complex in flavours, and as doughy as it can be refined. One could be forgiven for thinking such a sauce has no place on a Thanksgiving plate. One would be missing a great and comforting delight.

Turkey-Bacon was to be our fourth course; fifth, were we to take into account Chef's *amuse-bouche* sent out upon our seating. My only fear was that this hearty lamination of meats, dressing and sauce would lay us low before dessert and its advertised preview course. That fear was well founded, but we rallied. We even did most of the scullery's work by cleaning our plates as if ploughing the fields and tending the herds had been our immediate preoccupation rather than sleeping away the afternoon or getting our toes painted.

Sated by not only the kitchen's laudable efforts but also the wonderful bottles our sommelier dug from the recesses of the cellar, we three retired to yet another cavernous fireplace crackling with fiery logs. After nearly a month smelling only turf or coal on the grate, the spicy nose and popping hiss of a wood fire was pleasing and almost foreign. I was becoming accustomed to things which were new and revelling in those to which I was previously accustomed. In hindsight then, it shouldn't have been strange at all when coffee and fine old Irish malt shared in these ancient surrounds with two women who had been such an important part of my life turned flirtatious.

A dram became a decanter, logs became embers and we began saying 'goodnight' to the dining room staff as they left for the night.

The maître d'hôtel came to ensure we had everything we required. He had been our table captain on my first stay at the castle two years earlier when I visited with my parents on their first trip to Ireland. We assured him that we had surpassed any 'requirements' hours before. Genuine conversation ensued, and before I knew it, he was taking us into the Royal Suite, where just the previous summer the American president and his wife had stayed in advance of a major economic summit meeting.

Nothing makes one feel much more welcomed in a place that is far beyond one's station in life than a private tour of the best rooms in the house. I, therefore, made a mental note to let staff know they needed to charge me and refill the president's decanter as I replaced it with the empty I'd carried from our fireside table two floors below.

16

One-Way Hire

LITTLE IS AS IMPORTANT to a body the morning after a six-course Thanksgiving meal as a hearty breakfast. Well, I'll actually admit that I needed something. Even six courses couldn't soak up the two sherries and three bottles of wine we split and the thankfully uncounted shots of whiskey of the night before.

The castle's buffet included fruits of the season as well as dried/stewed renditions of the out-of-season varietals. There were breakfast cereals and pastries fresh from the oven. I'm pretty sure we'd seen the bakers coming into the kitchen as we were finding our way to our rooms. And lastly, cheeses from local farms, and Limerick ham – one of the great joys of Irish cuisine.

A question one does not expect to hear as the wait staff is clearing the remains of the second pot of coffee and dusting scone crumbs from the tablecloth is, 'And what would you like for your cooked breakfast?'

The castle's Irish breakfast appeared to have a cold course followed by à la carte selections that ranged from a full traditional breakfast with local black pudding – the pride of County Clare – or Irish beef hash with spuds grown on the property to poached wild salmon, or my favourite, lightly smoked, paprika-hued kippers with local eggs. Not that I needed, wanted, or should have had the second course. Still, the girls were slow to rise, and I wasn't looking forward to moving from the table – or anywhere, really – in the foreseeable future. Like a sailor on his second night of shore leave, I rallied when the two companions finally descended to the dining room and requested hair of the dog in the form of Bloody Marys. I decided not to mix my liquors. Few enough hours had passed between my last dram and now that anything other than whiskey would be mixing, so I ordered a drop for my coffee.

I also took advantage of the fuzzy memory of absconding with the president's stash and requested that the cost be added to my bill.

'Oh, Mister Gleason, our maître has already taken care of that. Said it was his pleasure, and he was happy to see ye three having such a fine time.'

Not only did we drink the president's whiskey … we drank it for free.

I do love that place.

❧ ❧ ❧

Leaving Sadie with the gamekeeper just a little while longer, we loaded ourselves and their luggage into the skate-ball bag for one last trip in the abomination of a car. Dogs being strictly forbidden in hired cars, I didn't want to jeopardise my already precarious positioning with Your Man down at the rental desk.

The trip to the airport for Sheri and Bridgett was a good time to replace the skate-ball bag before ongoing chiropractic care would be needed. Also, my next trip planned for Shannon was a few days beyond the twenty-eight days, going over which would apparently land me on Interpol's most-wanted list. So, we three set off for the airport: the return flight for them, a replacement car for me and the beginning of my first spell alone with Sadie since my parents had landed just days after my arrival.

The usual hugs and tears were usurped by the things one must focus on when travelling: which side of security to buy your €12 bottle of water, where to stop to get your VAT refunded, how to find out if the layover in Chicago is long enough to make the connection … those kinds of things. I left the two in a state of pre-travel hysteria and swung the skate-ball bag into the rental return lot.

Planning on another 28-day hire, I had to be picked up off the floor when Martin quoted me the price. (I didn't want to familiarise myself with him enough for him to become 'Your Man'.) Not only was it more than I was expecting to pay for a month's hire, Martin was about to charge me more than I had been e-quoted for my entire three-month stay. Seeing that smelling salts were nearly in order, an older and sure-footed woman came to my rescue, albeit speaking in hushed tones with a wandering eye for eavesdroppers.

'Take a one-way hire to Kerry Airport,' she said, 'just for a week or so. I'll text the manager down there and we'll get you set right.'

With that, she backed away slowly, as if our conversation had never happened. Part of me wondered if it really had. She disappeared behind a door I hadn't noticed before and I did not see her again. I had to wonder if, like the walking stick that made itself known when I was in need, she was sent to help.

Two weeks' hire was all I could get at my old and I still thought 'contracted for' rate. Kerry Airport in Farranfore was a MUCH shorter drive, only about fifty minutes or so, than the six-hour-plus Shannon round trip. Your One may not only have saved me money, but also a rather significant portion of my remaining months might be added back on to the visit. I had a lilt in my step as I walked out of the rental shed. Only the right, however, as my left leg was beginning to drag. So much so, in fact, that I stopped and did a quick calculation of how much Your One had just saved me. I spun around and asked for an automatic transmission upgrade. (All right, I carefully made a three-point-turn with cane in one hand and the rental shed's wall in the other.) If the kerb from which I had been about to descend was a worry, I could not imagine having to work a clutch on my trip back to the castle to fetch Herself and then back down to Kerry.

We shortened the rental to a week – as the fairy lady had suggested in the first place – and even with the one-way fee, I wasn't out any more money than Your Man must have saved me on the decanter of malt.

The Acne Carriage that awaited me in the appointed slot made me, once again, happy that I'd be turning it around in shorter time than expected. What was it with me and Irish rental cars?

17

Hardships and Hospitality

WINTER HAD SET ITSELF down for a long stay in the preceding days and I guess the warm log fires and deep crystal decanters had kept the cold at bay. The clouds seemed lower and hued between slate and gunmetal at times as Sadie and I drove along the shore road into The Town. My mood was also beginning to darken as I used the drive time to begin some financial calculations.

This winter's trip, less than a month in, was costing me significantly more than I had budgeted. Increased rental fees for the car and the impromptu Thanksgiving gift of the castle stay to the girls were expenses I'd not even thought about, let alone planned for. With another round of guests on their way in a few days, I had to do some serious cypherin'.

Other expenses were also beginning to reveal themselves as higher than expected.

There were times, with three women in the house and all, during which the electric power-shower in the bathroom had run for nearly two hours straight. I couldn't blame those with the longer hair. Water pressure through the thing was barely enough to rinse lather from my short hair. The girls had to stand under it with the nozzle practically pressed into their hair to get it clean. Electricity was not included in my rent, and I was beginning to see that my bills might soon outstrip my means.

Taking a page from the playbook of a friend's private pub in Canada, I decided that a voluntary 'House Fund' jar might help. Things like the utilities, toilet paper, laundry detergent, stuff everyone was using but wasn't covered in my rental agreement, could be helped along with a few bob from my guests. Food didn't seem to be much of an issue, as I was doing all of the cooking and everyone seemed very happy to kick in for the groceries. Rounds took care of themselves when it came to pub time, so I hoped people wouldn't mind a contribution to the fund.

My mood was beginning to brighten to a more heron-like hue even as the sky's colour was deepening with the approach of evening. All of that changed as I unlatched the Dutch door and Sadie scampered past me into The Cottage. A cold escaped the room and washed over me like the descriptions I've read of the presence of evil spectres. I'll not deny that I may have checked my door knocker to see if Jacob Marley's face might be there.

A step into the room and I felt as if I'd walked into an ice cave on a warm summer day. The heat seemed to be sucked from my body, and it was noticeably far colder inside The Cottage than out. Though Sheri and Bridgett had floated a few stories at the castle about sensing The Cottage might be haunted, I wasn't buying the idea. The whole place was cold and I was sure a good fire and cranking up the boiler would do the trick.

I didn't even remove my coat and gloves but went right to the fireplace, cold now from nearly three days of disuse, and lit the torn pages of the local phone directory, which caught the sticks and in turn lit the turf. I'd wait to load the whole thing down with a bucketful of coal until the turf had a good glow on. Heat began to emanate from the grate, but it seemed to suck cold air right past me faster than the warmth came to me. I furniture- and wall-walked my way into the kitchen where the old boiler stood cold. Cooler temperatures are typically better for my MS than warm, but the morning's forewarning of symptoms on my left side had only been exacerbated by the hours in the stupid little car I was driving. One hand on either furnishing or bulkhead was required, for my cane was still in the car, as was my luggage. I'd have to remember to bring that in.

The timer dial, which, not unlike a plug-in lamp timer, has small slots and clips that can be altered in order to adjust on/off times, read the incorrect time. It was several hours off. That was the first sign of trouble with the heating system. Suspecting that The Cottage had lost power while I was away, I checked the ice cube tray in the freezer.

There's an old trick my grandmother, my father's mother, taught me to check if the power has gone out while you're away on a trip. Mind you, this was needed before the days of digital clocks on every appliance and plug-in electric alarm clocks. The Cottage was furnished as if it were from that time, so I'd figured it was not a bad idea owing to the precarious state of everything else in The Cottage.

You simply place the ice cube tray upside-down in the freezer before you leave the house. Were the power to go out, for days even, and then come back on, you'd never know. Things could get cold and refreeze even if they thawed during an outage. If you flipped the tray over, any melted ice would fall from the tray and run to the bottom of the freezer.

Power didn't seem to be the case. The tray was fully frozen and quite intact.

I messed with the pilot switch, thinking that maybe it needed to be reignited, but that didn't seem to be the issue either. Finally I decided to check the large plastic bladder that was The Cottage's oil source to see if it was empty. Grabbing my cane from the car, but once again, not my luggage, I found plenty of oil in the tank.

What then could be the cause?

I've never been the 'mechanically inclined' sort; 'mechanically declined' might better describe me. Inclined or not, I knew that I did not have it in me to walk or drive down to the landlord's B&B for assistance right then. Sure a kip would refresh me. I'd head down and make the report when I went to resupply the nearly emptied cupboards. For now, I had a fire to take the chill off, and I was knackered.

I opted for the sofa in front of the fire rather than making an arduous ascent up the back stairs that I could not guarantee to my mind's satisfaction. And besides, my bedroom was likely to be frigid. I loaded the grate with a few scoops of coal and was even more tired for the effort. Lying down, I felt each and every lump in the decades-old divan and its cushions. No real matter, as I only remember Sadie giving me a quick sniff and curling herself in the seat of the adjacent wing-backed chair before I fell asleep.

* * *

The time couldn't be rightly ascertained by my addled brain when I woke to a sound I'd never heard in my life. It was a sound no one had ever heard, for, to my knowledge and experience, it had never before been made.

As I was lying on my left side, Sadie was atop my right hip, barking.

Unlike the name-inducing 'boof' sound made by my first dog, Boofy, Sadie wound up into each bark with a gravelly and whirring growl that reminded me of the rattling sound my great-grandfather's dentures made as he ate corn from the cob. Her whole body seemed required to force the ensuing 'Brrrop!' of her juvenile bark. She seemed just as surprised as I to hear this sound emerge from within her. There was a purpose to her bark, however, and my groggy mind began to wrap itself around that thought.

The light coming from the window at the front of the room was more pronounced than when I had lain down and the fireplace was now devoid of any light, or for that matter, any warmth. I came to the conclusion through my mental fogbank that I must have slept the night rather than the quick kip I thought I required. There was no telling how late it might be. Although it was brighter out, the light coming in was still grey. I was sure that Sadie's outburst was a combination of the lack of last night's supper and the need for her morning repast; that, and the fact that she'd last had a pee just before entering the icy Cottage uncounted hours earlier. The warm spot on my side, the only thing warm about me if I thought about it, led me to believe she'd spent a considerable amount of the night perched there. A bit of noise, audible even to me, started her next round of canine objection and I decided to help her investigate.

With every intention in the world of gently holding Herself up as I first sat and then stood from my semi-foetal, reclined position, the whole thing went awry. My left arm failed to answer the call and my right overcompensated. Sadie tumbled first to the sofa cushion and then to the floor. I immediately felt the dual fear of having broken my puppy's back and coping with an arm that was once again, as during my diagnosis, paralysed by MS.

Both fears were quickly allayed. Herself simply rolled over and took the boost as a cue to run to the door and bark, and my arm exhibited the familiar pins-and-needles of a limb regaining consciousness. My leg, to the contrary, did not simply feel as if it had fallen asleep. The sluggish and loppy limb felt no pins, no needles nor quite anything else. From mid-thigh it was as if I had only ragged attachment to the rest of the limb. My leg, below the thickest part, might have been a dead stick surrounded only with livery-feeling flesh wrapped too tightly with cellophane. It was a dead weight that sent a shockwave up my keep when it was placed down on the floor.

It was easier and less distracting – if a bit more cumbersome – to simply drag the uncooperative bough, rather than arduously lift and drop, as I followed Sadie to the door.

My current state made the sight of my landlord wrangling sheep from the garden into a trailer hitched to his car more welcome than I could have imagined. The sight of 'her' sheep being manhandled into the wagon excited Sadie to the point of exacting a frozen stance while several hours' worth of urine puddled on the ground around her. We watched him load the last of the ewes in and latch the tailgate before summoning Your Man forth into our ice palace.

After tracing the few things I had checked the night before, he assured me that he could have 'the boiler man' round to have a look.

'Have ye turf for the fire to warm this place up until I can get him around?' he asked. He must have felt the same heat-sucking cold though which Sadie and I passed our night's slumber.

'I've half a bag of coal, but that's about it,' I said. Pointing to my leg, whose foot was at a nearly right angle to its proper placement, I added, 'And with this old thing acting dumber 'n dirt, I don't see the Garda taking well to me driving into town for more.'

Arrangements were made for him to bring up a couple of bags of turf for the hearth. He even offered some soup The Princess had been cooking before he set off to take the ewes to a barn. A cold wind was forecast for the next few days, so he wanted to get the pregnant gals into some shelter. I only hoped that Sadie's and my shelter would soon feel warmer than it did. I'd been in winter barns warmer than The Cottage, and who knew how long the boiler man might take?

* * *

Soup and turf did make their way to The Cottage, and it's a good thing. It took several days for the boiler man to get around to the task and then there was the ordering of parts and scheduling of his return visit. The Princess and Your Man, however, did what they could to keep Sadie and her crippled up Da warm and fed.

Now, don't get me wrong: the temperature in the sitting room where I camped for the next several days never reached double figures. Blankets and the most inadequate electric space heater I've ever seen picked up the fireplace's flanks, and I wasn't up for much other than sleeping anyway. Nearing the week's end, the boiler was up and running, though it took several more days of running it full-throttle, 24/7 to take the chill from the stone wall. And though far from 100 per cent, my leg was beginning to respond – albeit slowly – to commands.

That then is how my first month in the wilds of Kerry drew to a close – cold and alone and suffering from multiple sclerosis. It wasn't, metaphorically speaking, much different from when I'd left Seattle. I was, however, learning of the simple kindnesses that make the hard times manageable. Soup, bread and an extra blanket can ease the difficulties just as they do those of a child … just as they have for centuries in this land of hardships and hospitality.

Sadie and I were going to be fine. Better than fine, because even though all we could seem to muster was enough energy to eat a bit now and again and sleep the rest of the time, we were together and we were home … and it was several days before we had to play host to another guest. But they would come soon enough.

(*Top left*) Trevis with Multi-Star Chef Roger Vergé at Cornell University's School of Hotel Administration, 1996; (*above right*) with luminary chef Madeline Kamman at Cornell University, 1997; (*opposite*) and, as a young apprentice, with famed French chef Pierre Franey at the New England Culinary Institute in Vermont, 1990.

PART III
The Journey: Favourite Recipes

18

Baking Recipes

NOW, I WOULDN'T BE much of a host if I didn't offer a few recipes to go along with the tales of my winter in Kerry.

Food has always been an important part of my life, from the days of my youth when our city's annual festival of the arts brought out the bit of diversity that seemed hidden from me the rest of the year round. I can still remember the sense of wonderment and travel as we'd sample tastes from the tents of small churches of ethnicities different from those I saw in my everyday juvenile life.

Native American soup filled with bits of bison fat and reconstituted hominy (an ancient type of maize first soaked in slaked lye then dried, oft used by Native Americans of the south-west desert), Vietnamese spring rolls – so much smaller and more exotic than the fat and watery versions one might find at a local Chinese buffet – even Lebanese sfiha (something of a cross between a vol-au-vent and a pizza), and the Greek Orthodox Church's mouth-watering souvlaki (skewers of marinated meat barbequed over charcoal in troughs erected in the street) were in abundance at this local event. Although, when the locals found out that they'd been queuing around the block for lamb, of all things, the church was obliged to switch to chunks of pork shoulder. Some things were just 'too foreign' for my home town, even at a cultural festival.

The first recipe I offer is for that 'perfect' scone for which I waited at the Shannon airport café. It's not exactly the version of the scone they served me. This is my own derivation of the simple staple found in every bakery and shop in Kerry and on most B&B breakfast boards. The type of dried fruit (and nuts, if you like) can be varied to what is on hand or can be 'poshed up' for company. Orange zest and dried sour cherries is a company favourite of mine, for example.

Stick to the recipes until you're familiar with them. Also, know that the brand of flour you use, the humidity of the day, and even the fat content of your buttermilk may cause the need for slight changes. I once used a flour in Ukraine that needed nearly twice the liquid called for in my recipes. Whatever you do, bake them soon and bake them often. They only stay fresh for about a day. Cheers!

—— *Buttermilk Scones* ——

Yields 8–12 scones
(depending on size and thickness)

240g/8½ oz/2 cups plain flour (plus extra for dusting)

6g/1 teaspoon baking soda

3g/1 teaspoon cream of tartar

50g/1¾ oz/¼ cup sugar

1.5g/¼ teaspoon table salt (preferably not iodised)

30g/1 oz/2 tablespoons cold butter (cut into ½ teaspoon-sized chunks)

60g/2 oz/½ cup dried fruit (currants, cherries, raisins, etc.)

180ml/6½ fl oz/¾ cup + 2 tablespoons buttermilk (plus extra for brushing if you like)

Method

Preheat oven to 220°C/425°F/Gas 7 and adjust rack to middle of the oven.

Stir all dry ingredients into a large bowl.

Add butter, toss to coat with flour and 'rub' the butter into flour with your hands until it resembles sand (a few larger flat, raggedy pieces of butter left are fine).

Toss dried fruit in flour mixture to distribute evenly.

Make a well in the centre of flour and add buttermilk.

Mix together using the broad side of a table knife until a soft dough just forms and turn out onto a lightly floured surface.

Gently form into a round, about 2 cm/¾ inch thick, being careful not to over-work.

Cut into scones using a 5–6 cm/2–2½ inch round cutter or drinking glass. Re-form the dough and cut one more time, but no more.*

Place on a lightly floured baking sheet and brush with buttermilk. (You can lightly sprinkle with sugar as well, if you like.)

Bake for 15–20 minutes until light golden-browned and nicely risen.

Cool for 2 or 3 minutes and serve warm.

Serve as you like, but unsweetened whipped cream and whiskey-orange marmalade is my favourite – recipe on p. 297.

* The pieces left after the second cutting can be broken into equal sized chunks and baked on a separate baking sheet. It is important not to work the dough more than absolutely necessary, as it will toughen and incorporate the butter too far into the dough for a proper rise in the oven. We used to call these 'Dog Bone Scones' in culinary school because the shape of them looked like a cartoon dog treat.

🖋 🖋 🖋

Breakfast, I learned quickly, was a meal that everyone ate when they stayed with me in Ireland; even if they weren't 'breakfast eaters'. Scones and breads were a staple in the house, but these self-raising pancakes became a favourite. Firstly, who doesn't like a good pancake? For me, however, the ease with which I could whip them together, coupled with their adaptability to be sweet or savoury and to use leftover bits from the fridge made them a go-to dish.

This recipe may be a bit more Scottish than Irish, I'm told, as they use milk and baking powder rather than buttermilk and baking soda as liquid and leavening. It matters not to me whence they came. You'll find them reason enough to have self-raising flour on hand (or make it, as you'll see in the note).

~~~~~~

—Self-Raising Pancakes—

Serves 2

115g/4 oz/1 cup self-raising flour*

60g/2 oz/⅓ cup granulated sugar

Pinch table salt

1 egg, beaten

Milk to mix

Method

Mix dry ingredients in a small bowl.

Stir in the beaten egg.

Fold in enough milk to create a batter to your liking. (The thicker the batter, the thicker your pancakes will be. You can thin this almost as much as crêpe batter, but not quite.)

Heat a griddle or non-stick pan with a bit of oil or butter over medium heat.

Drop the batter in 2–3 tablespoon sizes and cook until small bubbles rise to the top and begin to burst.

Turn pancakes and cook for another 2–3 minutes.

Serve warm with butter, jam, whipped cream (or my favourite, whiskey/blood orange marmalade syrup – recipe on p. 297).

Variations

I like to fold lots of different things into this batter to change it up. Cooked and chopped bacon, ham, or even leftover roast chicken can be fun. Sliced scallions, shredded courgette that has been drained for a bit or grated carrot are nice vegetarian options. Feel free to reduce the sugar by half if you are going for a more savoury pancake.

* Self-raising flour can be made at home if you don't have it on hand and keeps well for a couple of weeks. Simply mix together 2 cups plain flour, 1 teaspoon table salt and 1 tablespoon baking powder and store in an airtight container.

Basic soda bread came to the island, like many of the good things in life, by necessity. The Irish had only poor-quality 'soft' wheat with which to work and, as they were busy farmers, little time with which to work it into bread. This soft wheat flour doesn't take well to the long kneading and multiple fermentations needed to make yeast-raised breads. With the use of the commonly available chemical leavening agent, baking soda, and the necessary acid for the chemical reaction in the form of buttermilk, a cook could turn low-quality wheat flour into a nicely risen and sturdy loaf in a fraction of the time needed for yeasted breads.

Today, soda bread (in its white and wheaten forms) is still found on nearly every menu and on most kitchen tables in Ireland. While more traditional recipes use only flour, salt, soda and buttermilk that are baked in free-formed loaves, I offer you this variation. A little bit of sugar and a touch of fat, in the form of butter for greasing the loaf tin, turn this staple into something worth having on the table even if the lace cloth has been brought out.

Like the scone recipe, the amount of buttermilk needed will vary depending on several factors, including humidity of the day and the flour you've purchased.

— White Soda Bread —

Yields two 450g/1 lb loaves

500g/18 oz/4 cups plain flour

14g/2¼ teaspoons baking soda

4g/1⅛ teaspoon cream of tartar

5.5g/1 teaspoon table salt

50g/2 oz/¼ cup sugar

500ml/16 fl oz/2 cups buttermilk (plus more if needed)

Butter (for greasing the tins)

Method

Preheat oven to 220°C/425°F/Gas 7 for at least 30 minutes.
Sift flour, soda and cream of tartar into a large bowl. Stir in salt and sugar.

Make a well in the centre of the flour and pour most of the buttermilk into the well.

Stir with a wooden spoon until a spongy dough forms. Add more buttermilk if needed. Dry dough makes for hard loaves.

Grease two 450g/1 lb loaf tins well with butter.

Divide dough into the prepared tin, spreading with wet fingers but leave the surface a bit rough.

Place loaves on a baking sheet and put into the preheated oven, turn temperature down to 200°C/400°F/Gas 6 and bake for about 20–30 minutes.

Turn the loaves out of the tins and onto pan.

Lower oven temperature to 165°C/325°F/Gas 3 and continue to bake for another 10–15 minutes, until lightly brown and crusty.

Remove loaves to a rack (wrap in a kitchen towel for 15 minutes if you want a softer crust to the loaves) and cool completely before slicing.

🖋 🖋 🖋

Finally, a recipe that is both dear to my heart and coveted by family members and friends for years. The brown version of soda bread is sometimes known as wheaten bread in the North, whence my family came. It can be the coarser and less-refined cousin to white soda bread. This particular recipe is far from coarse and is very refined.

I made batches of the dry ingredients for this wheaten bread once per week during my winter in Kerry. I'd fill my ziplock bags with pre-measured dry ingredients when no one was in The Cottage or very early in the mornings, before guests were stirring. This allowed for quick mixing with the recipe far from the felonious eyes of those looking to garner 'my' secret.

The fact of the matter is that I am not stingy with my recipes. After years of teaching at various culinary schools and universities around the world, sharing recipes is just part of the fun of cooking and teaching. This particular recipe, however, was given to me in the strictest confidence by a most charming innkeeper very near my ancestral village. The woman is called Joan and her bed and breakfast, The Willowbank House in Enniskillen, County Fermanagh, was where Beth and I spent a night on my first trip 'home'.

We were the only guests the evening we stayed, but Joan and her husband Tom made us feel more than very welcome in their home. Our breakfast there is still one of the most memorable of the trip. Beth fell in love with the scones we had our first morning in Cork city. I, on the other hand, was besotted with Joan's version of the simple brown bread. When I almost apologetically asked if I might have her recipe, acknowledging that I'd most assuredly understand if she'd want to keep something as special as this bread to herself, she thought about it for a moment and then pleasantly declined.

I understood, of course. From the awards and citations on the entry foyer walls, I could tell that Joan was very proud of her accomplishments as an innkeeper and cook. We made it our job to enjoy the slices before us and savour them in our memories until what would have to be an imminent return. Seriously: this bread was worth the trek all the way to the North.

Both Beth and I were thrilled when Joan returned to the table a bit later in our breakfast with a plate heaped with more slices of her wheaten bread. That she also had a neatly typewritten recipe along with the plate sent me over the top.

'Ye must promise me that you'll not be giving this out or be writing it in a cookbook,' she emphasised, before handing over the crisp sheet of white typing paper.

I made my solemn vow to keep her venerated formula between just the two of us and to the day this book was first published, it remained that way. You can ask my mother; she's been after the damned thing ever since. It is only with the gracious permission of this most generous woman that I offer Joan Foster's take on Irish wheaten bread. Even my mother did not see the recipe before *Chef Interrupted* was published.

–Joan Foster's Irish Wheaten Bread–

Yields two 450g/1 lb loaves

350g/12 oz/3 cups coarse wholemeal flour

200g/7 oz/1½ cups plain flour

12g/2 teaspoons baking soda

25g/2 tablespoons sugar

1 pinch table salt

30g/1 oz butter, cut into 8 pieces (plus more for greasing the tins)

500ml/1 pint buttermilk (plus more if needed)

Method

Preheat oven to 220°C/425°F/Gas 7 for 30 minutes.

Stir flours and soda together in a large bowl to fully combine.

Stir in sugar and salt to mix.

Rub butter into the flour mixture with the palms of your hands to incorporate.

Make a well in the centre and add buttermilk.

Stir with a wooden spoon until a thick, porridge-like consistency (more buttermilk may be needed, depending on flour).

Pour into two lightly buttered 450g/1 lb loaf tins and smooth dough with wetted fingers.

Place tins on a baking sheet and into the preheated oven. Turn temperature down to 200°C/400°F/Gas 6 and bake for 20–25 minutes.

Lower oven temperature to 165°C/325°F/Gas 3, turn loaves out onto a baking sheet and bake for an additional 5–10 minutes.

Cool on a rack for 20–30 minutes.

PART IV

December

19

The Feast of the Immaculate Deluge

CHRISTMAS HOOPLA doesn't begin in The Town until the Feast of the Immaculate Conception (hereafter 'the feast') during the second week of December.

Father Christmas does not make his entrance during the Macy's parade. No Thanksgiving holiday heralds the unofficial opening of the retail season. Shopkeepers do not begin with the yuletide bullshit while still restocking shelves with Halloween candy. But when it starts … Look out!

Not a shop, pub, market or emporium goes unadorned, or rather un-over-adorned.

The days prior to the feast must be magic for the children, as everyone everywhere seems to haul dusty boxes, bags and bundles of gaudy decorations from unseen storage. Lights are tested, torn bits repaired with tape or glue, and a place made for holly and a tree. And when you consider that the feast is fewer than three weeks from The Father Christmas Show, seeing the decorations having their annual once-over must make it seem like the most *magical* magic.

The town and county council's men are out and about with their Cherry Pickers, hanging ornamentation plucked straight from any small American city *c.*1955.

The Town boasts every lamp post and telephone pole bedecked with large silver-fringed snowflakes, each with either a gold bell, silver ball or an oversized red candle wired to its centre.

The kicker is a pair of Soviet-era loudspeakers perched at either end of the main street just far enough to ensure an overlap of dozens of yards where both can be heard. The three-second delay between them makes one feel even more as if you've stepped through a time portal and gotten caught in some Celtic wrinkle.

Nowhere else in the western world are the paper chains I remember making as a young boy considered acceptable decoration for a business the way they are in The Town.

It all lends a charm, and I don't know, 'realness' to the place. The Town isn't putting on Dublin airs, trying to be some place it's not. The sense that Reb Tevye, albeit as a Catholic, dressed in a knitted jumper and wool cap, could dance through The Town singing is not out of the question here. Family, God and the GAA: that's Tradition, and tradition is what's important in The Town. It keeps things on an even keel even when disaster strikes.

🖋 🖋 🖋

The rain had begun, in fits and starts, a few days prior – nothing unusual, as I was beginning to realise. It must have hit its stride just before I woke Herself to have her morning piddle after my 2.30 a.m. shower to ready for the next airport run. We'd found it within ourselves to move up to the bedroom a few days earlier, and though I'd not yet driven as far as Shannon, I had made it up to Kerry airport to swap out the rental car for a monstrosity I called 'The Tank'. I'd even begun to shower on a regular basis, which was saying something. There was no wind in this storm. It was as if the clouds had simply parked over The Cottage and the angels collectively unzipped, after a night down the pub, to relieve themselves en masse.

Having not yet mastered the art of the quick pee, I was surprised by Sadie's turnaround time. Still, even though we had been out less than five minutes and I stood in as much of a lee as The Cottage could offer, I had to change all the way down to my underwear for the soaking we got.

Herself warmed and dried in front of the coal, which I had dumped on the grate before my shower, and appeared angry and aglow while I shifted my wardrobe. I thumped down the stairs, freshly clad but still smelling reminiscent of a wet ewe, and found Herself splayed out on her fleece, auburn-hewed in the firelight, in her default sleeping posture – a seal on its belly with one foreleg folded back like an errant flipper. I found out later that her grandmother, Trudy, whom she looks so very much like, sleeps this way, too.

'Let's get under way, Newkdara!' was all I had to say and she bolted for the door, leaving her warm, fireside fleece for my old jumper in the back window of the freshly acquired Hire-a-Tank.

Rain was coming straight down and harder than when we had first gone out, if that's possible to imagine. A two-foot fog seemed to rest all around as we lurched into the dark laneway, but it was really the raindrops bouncing back off the pavement or in the flats and hollows, splashing from the surface of puddles ever deepening into pools. We surfed down the hill into The Town. I noted flotsam in our headlights speeding past us as the overflowing lane-side gullies washed seaward faster than second gear would take us.

The town was newly decorated. This early morning being the day after the feast, the shopfront windows were alight with a combination of coloured, sometimes flickering, fairy lights and strings of bare bulbs like those I remember from Christmas tree lots in front of groceries and filling stations when I was young. We bolted as if catapulted out of the last roundabout and headed northwest, and I could see in my rearview that an incoming tide was colliding with cumulative waters rushing down from the surrounding hills.

We would return to a much different scene.

* * *

Heading up to Shannon, we drove through ever larger loughs of standing-cum-rushing water. We entered The Other Larger Town a bit shy of two hours after watching the tide meet the mountain-borne torrent. The drive normally took just past three quarters of an hour, but dodging the wash-deposited boulders in the dark of a very early morning slowed my progress markedly.

Here, where an honest-to-god river divides The Other Larger Town and meets the sea, anti-flooding precautions are a centuries-old infrastructure. The system of canals, flood breaks and natural, sponge-like marshes along with builders who knew better than to erect in a floodplain kept houses and businesses out of the wash. Roads and bridges, however, seemed to be more a part of the water diversion scheme than protected by it.

The heft of The Tank I'd exchanged for my previous wind-up toy at Kerry airport just days earlier kept Sadie and me from being swept seaward as I navigated the dark roads. The currents we experienced brought to mind those I'd coxed ships through in the island passes of Alaska's Bering Sea. In order to concentrate fully on my duties as conning officer of this un-commissioned Irish Naval vessel, I had been driving us along sans the companionship of RTÉ radio. Finally pulling The Tank up a grade and past the Piper's House, I caught a glimpse of the fully outstretched Sadie in the rear window, and beyond her, the receding flood as the tide began to pull the influx of fresh water out to sea. I clicked on the receiver and waited for the archaic tank's radio vacuum tubes to warm.

What I heard come to life caused me to pull to the soft shoulder and listen – I'm fairly certain, slack-jawed – to the words of a song I've known for years.

I'd listened to 'Fairytale of New York' by Jem Finer and Shane MacGowan for years. I'd croaked out the words of the chorus – 'The boys of the NYPD choir / Were singing "Galway Bay" / And the bells were ringing out / For Christmas Day' – at the top of my lungs in cars and bars and at house parties for years of holidays. The Pogues' raucous, hard-driving music and Irish-accented punk approach to the song made the lyric seem fun and playful. Even a bouncy version by Christy Moore left my American mind humming the tune as if it were a musical romp and light of heart. Never, NEVER had I thought about the pain and hope and utter despair that were in the lyrics. Performed in spoken word by Gerry McArdle and Colette Proctor as an audio play, however, the voices put a lump in my throat and brought tears to my eyes.

On a ridge, out of the way of the flood and still several hours before the sun would lighten the blue-black to heather grey, I sat and wept as I heard two craggy, old and soon-for-the-grave voices recalling love and hope for each other and their adopted home of New York City.

Sadie and I were on our way to collect my nephew, who had spent two Christmas Eves dug into a hole in the deserts of Iraq with the 82nd Airborne Division of the US Army. If anyone had the right to relate to the sentiment of stolen dreams and unfulfilled promises, it was he and his mates.

🖋 🖋 🖋

The same storm that filled the Kerry sod to the tipping point also slowed air traffic over the Atlantic. The Nephew, only moments earlier having emerged from customs and immigration, was standing in line for a coffee when I entered the arrivals hall to greet him. As a young soldier he'd spent time in areas of the world where driving on 'the wrong side' was the custom, so I was happy to relinquish the helm to the young man and simply act as navigator. My legs and mind were still a bit weakened by my recent exacerbation.

We had the conversation about the driving responsibilities over breakfast in the airport café. It was hard to believe that more than a month and over a half-dozen trips to airports had already passed and that I was a full third into my stay. Ireland was becoming familiar, maybe a bit too familiar as to the amount of time on the airport runs, but I felt as if I'd only been playing the tour guide. Was I really living my dream of being a part of The Town, or was I simply the advance guard for the American tourist army and their successive waves of invasion forces?

Time had to be taken, as little was to be afforded, to see and experience the Ireland that I had come to see, not just the Ireland everyone wanted me to show them. Just as an overly rich sauce can be tempered with a few drops of acid in the form of lemon juice or vinegar, so too would I have to rein in some quiet, alone time for Sadie and me to be with the locals and in the locales.

It may have been the breakfast that brought the thought to me. I had for so many months longed for the taste of my first Irish breakfast here in that very café. Now that I'd had a chance to taste the rashers, hand-made black pudding and sausages of Mr Sheehy's butchery in The Town, I knew that so much more was behind the emerald curtain, were I to simply draw it back and step through. A writer must ferociously devour the prose of others as he reaches within himself for his unique voice. A chef, too, must dine upon the menus of distinguished colleagues and hash-slingers alike in order to enamour the palate.

Our overly salted bacon and sawdust-dry pudding set me to my new mission, my original mission, to not just visit this place but live here. That The Nephew wanted to use The Cottage and Kerry as a base for exploring the entirety of the island for the next three weeks, that MS was lessening its grip on my legs and my spirit, and that my current ride was a rental retread was actually going to afford me what I had thought I'd have to steal.

The Tank was years, quite possibly decades, older than The Nephew, but the rental that the fairy lady had put me in touch with gave me the best possible deal. There were a few dents and scrapes, but it was far larger than my budget would have afforded. It had the added benefit of fitting into the rural countryside around The Town. In fact, even as we drove through Limerick city and its environs, we may have been the target of a few 'country bumpkin' glances which I far preferred to the 'bloody tourist' stares.

Coming into The Other Larger Town from the north, we passed the spot where the rear-window-sleeping Sadie and I had stopped to listen to the formerly loving couple hiss love-filled insults at the only person who could ever love them. I thought about bringing up the topic of The Nephew's service in Iraq and was trying to create the appetiser course to such a conversation. You can't just plop a thick slab of prime rib roast on a plate, stick it in front of a person and call it dinner. Neither could the topic of the horrors of war be opened without at least some salad chat.

Before I could act as conversational *garde manger*, we came upon the clean-up efforts of the local fire brigade. Using high-powered hoses intended to extinguish blazes, the lads were blasting mud and the like off the streets and back down the dykes and embankments into the river and canals. With the help of county councilmen in wellies and their brooms, shovels and assorted farm implements, the fire brigade of The Other Larger Town were well on their way to clearing the mess. Owing to the condition of The Town as we left, I decided it might be best to take the mountain road to The Cottage rather than the coast road. My description of the storm and Sadie's and my navigation of the same forestalled any talk of war with The Nephew. The Town, thus the coast road, had been hit pretty hard by the storm, its run-off and the incoming tide. The water had reached the streets and buildings of town, and I later learned that the coast road had several washouts. While the mountain road had a few rocks and the occasional tuft of an adjoining field or meadow in it, we didn't have to negotiate the sodden and freshly discarded furnishings of homes and businesses in the floodwater's path.

Knackered from the early rise and long journey, I excused myself for a late morning kip while The Nephew settled in. I encouraged him to venture into town for a look around. I'd plan to meet him in one of the pubs for a pint. It would be the first time I'd drunk with the young, now legal, man. I looked forward to it. He asked if Sadie could come along with us to the pubs and I couldn't rightly answer.

Yet another reason I needed some time in The Town to just poke about. There must be a few pubs that would welcome us two, the poser and his dog, but even a month into the stay, I couldn't yet say which.

20

Ionad Páirceála

AFTER ANAESTHESIA-LIKE sleep through to the late afternoon, I put the kettle on for tea and made Sadie her supper. The sky had become tarnished from silver to pewter during my kip. The day was passing and the low clouds darkened with every passing minute of the long waves of winter light. Still, they were lighter and brighter than when The Nephew and I had descended the mountain road hours earlier.

The kettle had boiled but the teapot was not yet scalded when a rapping at the Dutch door announced the return of our guest.

Soaked to the waist and mudded beyond his shins, The Nephew was removing his trousers when I opened the door. Months of desert bivouacking had flushed the Pacific Northwest modesty from the young man – not that anyone could see for the hedgerow-cum-forest that surrounded our gardens. Shouted explanation from the top of the stairs told of his coming upon the clean-up scene in town and how he simply picked up the nearest useful implement and dug in as needed.

As he wolfed down most of a box of Jaffa Cakes with his tea, which I'd spiked with sugar and whiskey rather than milk to stave off the chill, he named a roster of people he'd met and helped during his afternoon of relief work. Publicans, shopkeepers … he rattled off people I should have already known, people whose names I should have been able to recite. I must have let slip a lament of my state as tourist in residence. 'Jesus, no, Uncle!' he blurted through a cloud of Jaffa crumbs. 'They all knew who I was when I said I'd come to visit my uncle from America. Everybody said something nice about "The American and his Wheaten bitch". I thought they were talking about Aunt Sheri until I realised it was Sadie. "She's so soft to pet" was the giveaway.'

Here was proof positive that I needed to return the kindness of knowing the people who knew of me. We laughed and I opened another packet of McVitie's, skipping the tea and sugar in our mugs this time.

🐦 🐦 🐦

For better than a week, The Nephew would jump on a bus at The Town's only stop and head off for a day or two of Irish recon. From as far away as The Giant's Causeway on the far craggy coast of County Antrim in the North and the cosmopolitan streets of Dublin, he would show up at The Cottage every few days with a rucksack of dirty laundry and a story of the one that got away when it came to romantic endeavours. I'd feed and water the lad and offer suggestions as to what he might find interesting on his next quest.

The Nephew seemed to be searching for something from the outside to fill a hole or perhaps to reawaken some part of him he'd lost in the war. Though we never got around to actually discussing any of what he'd been through or what he was experiencing then, I could empathise with him.

Our worlds were much different. The intertwined hawser of the horrors he must have seen, the tasks required of him and the life his battles sucked from his soul made my issues seem like spider's floss. We were both searching for a way, a place, a person or an occupation to fill a 'hole'. The problem being that these holes are seldom filled with neatly shaped puzzle pieces.

Rather, the bits torn from our lives are jagged and irregular and often pull whole yarns from the tapestry into which they are woven. Multiple sclerosis had unravelled so much of my life that I was only now becoming aware of the extent of the damage. Ireland was my loom and The Town my shuttle. The places where I could find my broken threads and re-weave new experience and fresh insight into a blanket of life were not only worth keeping for myself, but for warming those around me. I hoped The Nephew could take the time in Ireland to unpack his cloth and see the rips and tears that he needed to patch.

🖋 🖋 🖋

Further into The Nephew's 'stay', which as I said was more of a come-and-go thing, my old pals Nigel and Joan arrived from California. Nigel's mum was from English/ Irish stock, so she had no issues naming her son Nigel. His prep-school mates had more of a go with the 'issue'; thus few of his friends call him that now. It was his old but never forgotten college love who brought his given name back into vogue among close friends after they reconnected in a most romantic manner of which I was unwittingly a part.

I'd more wittingly been a part of their unification as husband and wife. By request of the couple and with the assistance of the Internet, I became The Honourable (in name alone) Right Reverend Trevis L. Gleason in order to marry the happy couple. Joan is an attorney in … we'll call it the 'public sector', while Nigel holds a vice presidency at a small banking firm. That two citizens with such upstanding careers would have no one but me, a kilted preacher, ink still drying on his online ordination certificate, wed them tells you as much about this wonderful duo as it does about the special place we hold in one another's hearts. How we met is inconsequential. That we met, and have stayed close friends through nearly two decades, better than half a dozen moves, good times and bad, and from practically being neighbours to a distance of thousands of miles, is of utmost consequence. These are my people, and I theirs.

Fitting, therefore, that they would be the first visitors to benefit from my recent explorations into the places not actually hidden from the eyes of tourists, but rather passed over by those in search of something for which one needn't search.

The weather had chilled significantly in the weeks since MS grabbed hold of my legs and spirit. Even the pubs with roaring fires crowded with patrons in thick, damp jumpers gave off a chill borne from deep within the stones that constructed their walls. This ever-present state of semi-refrigeration kept my body's electrical system cool. I felt more energy than I actually had to spend. Once I was used to the real balance in my energy account, however, I was able to write cheques without overdrafting my body's ability to cover.

Sadie and I made good use of the reprieve and the time when we didn't have to play usher to the expected sights of Kerry. We took the turns we'd avoided, the roads off the main and used the Gazetteer and Key of our Ordnance Survey map of the area to guide us more than the roads illustrated ever could. The symbol for waterfall or the word 'ford' along a steam was reason enough for an outing. The most helpful hint our aptly named '*Sraith Eolais*' (Discovery Series) map offered was a little white 'P' inside of a small blue box.

'*Ionad Páirceála*' or 'Parking' made sense for such a symbol. The places we saw them sometimes made none.

Often, these Ps denoted nothing more than a wide spot in the road, occasionally not even that. Other times we would find actual car parks, but evidence of any recent tenancy by vehicles would require archaeological work to uncover. The most rewarding Ps we found came at the end of dirt and gravel roads. Sometimes these roads were no more than farm machine two-track boreens that turned off the unnamed roads that turned off the Regional roads that turned off the National roads.

It wasn't far from one such P that Herself and I, following not much more than an old sheep path, stumbled upon a small, village golf course. There was, predictably, an actual road (more the case of one of those two-tracks) to get to the links, but we hadn't yet come to that road. We were finding far too much enjoyment taking roads of our newly discovered symbol-driven tourism to simply follow the beaten path, even if the path was typically only beaten by the shit-spackled tractors of the sort I'd first encountered nearly a month and a half before.

Nigel, being both an avid golfer and of Irish descent far more recent than mine, had paid the extra cash to board his clubs on the plane and filled half his small suitcase with golf wear he'd considered appropriate for the season. I can only imagine that his was the only golf bag on the December flight to Dublin. It was his first trip to his ancestral island, which some say rivals in passion for the game only the neighbouring land of its purported origin. Nothing was going to stop him from hitting the course on at least one day of the visit, and the rain provided few such days of opportunity.

Much can be done on a soft day – the days when an upturned tin might fill with rain in a few hours. Little can be found to occupy the desperate days, which we'd suffered for most of Nigel and Joan's stay. Little, save acquainting oneself with a good book, a good pint and good craic – all of which can be found down at the local pubs. Now, don't get me wrong; little gives we three (and, on the occasion of The Nephew's brief re-entry into The Town's orbit, we four) much more pleasure than the smell of turf, the taste of Guinness and the sound of our own laughter coaxed by the ambiance of a local. Nigel, however, was champing at the bit to get out for a 'real' Irish golf experience. The course I'd found, and to which we'd all driven on the actual road designed for the journey this time, was exactly the type of course Nigel had hoped to play. Along with taking into consideration the occasional sand trap, local rules for ovine hazards must have applied to the course as well. On the occasion of our soggy trek to the links, no fewer than two dozen sheep could be counted tending to the fairways. With the crashing of waves on nearby cliffs to applaud a well-executed putt and the bleating of sheep in lieu of golf claps, playing the village eighteen offered the thrill of a Celtic Augusta for a few euro deposited into an honour box at the first tee.

All that was required now was a little moderation in the wind or the rain, preferably both, and he'd be in his version of heaven, with a scratch handicap.

I'd once enjoyed the game of golf myself – not that I was particularly good at it. I was once told by Sheri's brother that I had a 'natural swing', and that if I gave it time and attention I might make a decent player. I teed up my last round, or part of a round, after I'd 'recovered' from my diagnosing MS attack. On my second shot from the tee on our second hole I pulled back my club, and at the top of my swing with most of my weight on my weak side, collapsed into a heap.

I nearly rolled down the slope upon the crest of which my ball lay and into the water hazard above which it stood. Everyone in my foursome knew of my condition. 'Multiple sclerosis …' had been my answer, accompanied by a disarming chuckle, to 'What's everybody's handicap?' before we'd carted to that first tee. Carts converged on the scene of my uncoordinated folly. I drove our cart the rest of the way and that was my last time on a course.

The morning Nigel decided would be his day with the clubs wouldn't have been the day I'd have chosen even if I were still playing the game. Though lighter than previous mornings when he'd walk about the gardens and ruminate on the day's possibilities, the sky was still rent by torn clouds and the dusty, metallic smell of far-off, lightning-produced ozone stung my nose. With only a couple of days left and a Kerry weather forecast as reliable as a lame dog at a game of fetch, our duffer decided the day was as good as he might get and better than he was likely to get were he to wait.

Joan, Sadie and I opted for a morning romp on a nearby strand that was on her list anyway and far closer to the shelter of a pub where the ocean-born squalls make their way ashore. And they did …

It was easy enough for us to duck into the lee of a grass-topped dune when the wind-whipped rain skipped fistfuls of sea foam up the surf and over the glistening sand left by the receding tide. More than a few of these sea-marshmallows caught Sadie's attention and inspired her to tuck her tail and bum under her legs and bolt out after the skittering fluff. Catching the quarry would not have been in question had her growing aversion to rain not turned her around to head back to our sandy shelter.

It was only easy, however, because I habitually kept an eye on the sea, which availed us the time to get out of the way of the peppering spray. Nigel was trying to keep his eye on the ball and gauge the fickle gale's potential detriment to his iron shots. A driver would have lofted the ball into the wind high enough to carry the damned thing most of the way to Boston. He, pyjama-clad at the kitchen table, regaled us with stories of some of his more *Caddyshack*-esque moments – hunkered behind a rock or shrub and wondering how golf could have become an Irish pastime in the first place.

Dishing steak & Guinness stew from an earthenware crock I'd set in the cooker before our morning departure, I topped our bowls with heaps for roasted root vegetables that filled the kitchen with the fragrance of love and parsnips. It was no matter that the kitchen fireplace couldn't hold an ember. The heat of the oven, ardour of our bond, fervency from the second bottle of wine we'd opened and the sheer joy of a snoring puppy under our feet warmed us more than could a ton of coal.

🖋 🖋 🖋

The Nephew left the country on a Thursday, and I said goodbye to Nigel and Joan on the next Saturday. We'd the good fortune to hear a mutually favourite singing duo in Limerick city the night before they departed for Dublin. In America you see this group at large theatres and the occasional small arena. In Limerick, we gathered with about 300 fellow aficionados in a pub that offered around three times more room for patrons than it did for the band. I picked Sadie up on Sunday morning from her brief overnight with the Wendy Lady and headed toward home.

I actually thought of it as that word: home.

21

Half-time

STRIPPING THE BEDS OF their sheets and generally tidying up The Cottage, I looked at the guest-room calendars I'd posted on all the bedroom doors. I was happy to see that Sadie and I had five days before our next lodgers were to arrive. After that, all hell would break loose on the sleeping-arrangement front. Three rooms and a sofa would be stretched to hold as many as seven people. Only two of the seven, being a married couple, would prefer to sleep in the same bed, and none of the three groups of travellers had ever met.

That three of my affable transients were single women and my former colleague Joe was currently unattached created the potential that my charting and positioning of the sleeping arrangements would be an exercise of extreme over-preparation. Joe is also a chef, and even though he is six times more talented than I and at least a couple of times better looking, we were and are great pals. Odds were in favour of Your Man for having a better shot at a holiday shag than I. The inside track, however, would have revealed said handicap to be more because two of the three were my landladies back in Seattle and the third, a dear friend of theirs.

You don't sleep with the holder of your lease, and you don't do something stupid with her friend. Joe, however, understood another standing rule: you don't offer candy to just one person unless you've enough to share with the whole class.

As the larger bedroom would be better suited for the ladies, anticipating an air mattress at the very least, there was going to have to be some juggling around the time they arrived. I'd scheduled the married couple, the Trinkets, into the guest room for the first part of their stay and Joe into the bunk closet.

Once Cara, Hester, and Lorraine stormed The Cottage, however, the whole arrangement shifted. The Trinkets would move into my smaller room until the second week of January, when Mr Trinket would be part of the mass departure and Mrs Trinket would stay on for another couple of weeks. I'd shift to the second bunk in the closet with Joe, so that the 'Terrible Treble', as they would mockingly be called, could stack themselves into the largest chamber.

Moving from one room to the next on the first floor, I also noted an asterisk next to the date on my room's scheduling calendar. I couldn't remember the reason I might have marked my room with the symbol – not until sitting down for a simple supper of eggs and Mr Sheehy's sausages did it dawn on me why. I had reached the halfway point of my stay in The Town, the midpoint of a journey I'd dreamt of for decades, planned for months and burdened with unrealistic expectations.

The thought made for a melancholy meal even though the bangers had no rival in quality or flavour and the greengrocer had told me the name of the hens who laid my eggs the previous morning. I was alone when I left Seattle and alone when I arrived in Ireland. I was alone for nearly a week when MS came calling, and though I longed for alone time while tripping over one group of guests or another, I didn't enjoy being alone on the zenith of my adventure.

Alone wasn't something I'd experienced very much in my life, but it wasn't the aloneness that seemed to stick to me. In fact, I came to realise that I was, for the first time I could remember in my life, feeling lonely.

It is one of the great losses that I hear from people who, like me, live with multiple sclerosis: being taken out of, sequestered from, set aside by and excluded from society.

Within five months of my diagnosis, it was obvious to me and to my doctors that my recovery would not go as far as allowing me to continue my hectic job. I informed my employer and we developed a relatively speedy exit strategy. What was supposed to be a jolly retirement party ended up as more of a professional funeral for 'The Chef', with no one really knowing how to act on such an occasion, myself included. I was then simply unplugged from my former working life and my career's coffin lowered into the grave.

No longer was I to be called upon for consultation, assistance or information. No longer was I relevant, it seemed to me, and I spent a good number of months dangling my feet into the dark, swirling pool of self-doubt and despair. I often wondered if I could or would ever get up and continue my journey or if I'd just slip beneath the surface and never be heard from again. A bus full of commuters passes you on a busy street. A car idles, waiting for a traffic light to change. The azure-blue summer sky is unzipped by the contrail of a jumbo jet filled with hundreds of souls. An airplane on approach or departure comes close enough to the ground for us to see the ant-like scene below as it gets on with the workaday world … and they all have a story.

Have you ever thought of the lives going on inside that plane far, far above your head, the society thousands of feet below your airborne feet or in the commuter bus? Have you ever felt yourself cut off from the world as if you were in a personal capsule catapulting through time, space and dimension and nobody gets it … and the world still turns?

As we sit in our cars at a stoplight, the city moves and breathes and gets on with its life. We are, essentially, alone. Life with MS can be that way sometimes. A lot of times. I felt as though I was trying to find my footing halfway between arrival and departure.

We all – MS or not – move through the world in our own little spaceship. We interact with the world in our own way and the world with us. But no one can know the air we breathe inside our capsule. No one can understand completely the fears and hopes and worries and how I might be overjoyed to feel pain in my leg one day … because I haven't felt anything in that limb for a while.

There can be a sense of aloneness while living with MS that makes perfect sense to me. That does not mean I have to be lonely.

I don't think the amount of aloneness is the cause of a person feeling lonely. Even though I was thousands of miles and better than a day's travel from anyone who really knew me, I had felt more alone than this night. Sure, sitting singularly at a country table with five empty chairs on a dark country night far from all one loves or loved is solitude. I felt more alone with Sheri just one room away while I lay in an MRI chamber on the night of my diagnosis with multiple sclerosis. As great electromagnets spun the cells in my body in unison to face their artificial North, I realised that no matter how many people gather around us, none of them will ever be close enough to turn our bodies back when they determine to self-inflict damage.

It's no wonder that people living with MS not only experience symptoms of clinical depression more frequently than the general population but at a higher rate than people with other chronic and/or debilitating conditions. The chemical changes that happen in the brain as the immune system strips its wiring of protection may be part of the reason. That this damage can occur anywhere in the brain also means that our emotional centres can be compromised by the disease itself. The ironic slice of reality that tops the depression and MS sandwich is that the medications most commonly prescribed to modify the course of the disease are very well known to cause depression on their own.

It's no wonder as well, and a crying shame, that people with 'my' disease are as much as seven and a half times more likely to take their own lives than the general population.

Odd as it might sound, that very thought is what brought me out of my Halftime funk. In reading as much as I could the night after my first MRI and researching the drug choices available at the time of my diagnosis, I learned much about MS and depression and the suicide factor. It was the final factor that tipped the scales in favour of my first disease-modifying therapy; it had the lowest reported rates of suicide or 'suicidal thoughts'. Fighting MS is one thing. To have to fight against a drug that might rob me of more than the disease was already going to take was one battle I could avoid.

As if the thud of a second-half kickoff had been heard inside my skull, I snapped back to the present. I saw the dark night out the kitchen window not as a hollow void into which I might wander endlessly, but rather as dark and plush eiderdown that smelled of turf smoke, soft to the touch and soothing to the soul. The morning would bring not the last half but rather the joyous continuation of my journey. MS could (and might) take my legs again, and it sapped my energy at nearly every turn. I would not allow it even the slightest nibble at my spirit. Then, as if on cue, Herself sat up and shook off her post-supper sleep. We both shook it off and spent the evening in front of the television, turning it on for the first time since I'd arrived. A nature programme about tigers in India was on the only channel the set received. Sadie sat on my lap, very attentive, and watched the big cats' every move. I couldn't help but let slip my feelings from the adjoining room. If happiness, as Charles Schulz told my generation, is a warm puppy, said warm puppy watching television from your lap is pure bliss.

🐦 🐦 🐦

The Town had become markedly busier during the days leading up to Christmas. Not only were more tourists arriving and the local residents out and about in larger, more obvious throngs, but former residents, family members who'd moved to the cities or emigrated to all the corners of the world that fleeing Irish have populated for centuries, were descending on their home place as well. All around the streets and shops there was a bustle of old friends greeting one another and sharing gossip about this one or that. Who had arrived, who was expected and who wouldn't be able to make it home this year was on every busybody's lips, not to mention stories about what he or she might have done while away. All these were topics of lively conversation.

Christmas time is also the wedding season around many rural parts of Ireland. It's the time in the year when so many have returned home that it only seems fitting that this be the time for nuptial gatherings as well as the Christmas turkey. In towns and villages all over Kerry, large gatherings of cars around churches and unhappy children pressed into suits and dresses and hopped up on Lucozade and sweeties run about churchyards and hotel car parks while their smartly dressed parents are in attendance at some relative or friend's wedding. The children would rather be awaiting Father Christmas than the tossing of a bridal bouquet.

One such wedding party was posing for photos on the steps of The Town's Catholic church as Sadie and I passed by. I recognised the groom and two of his attendants as the lads who had made their way, howling in pain (I'd surmised) as much as in laughter, in and out of the surf where I'd taken Herself for a morning romp. Clad now in a starched shirt and blue suit rather than the swimming gear he was born in, Your Man looked as though the bracing thrash in the tide had done over the effects of the night before. He, along with his swimming mates, appeared ready for a rematch of the night that had left them in need of that swim. Shouts of congratulations and encouragement rang out from passers-by on foot and in cars, which slowed to a crawl to honk and wave at the happy couple. Traffic came to a complete halt when the

wedding party pulled up stakes and shifted headquarters
to the pub directly across the road from the church. The
day was as warm and bright as the smiles on the happy
couple's faces and the groom slapped me on the back as he
passed by, inviting me in for a drink.

'And your pup, too,' he said, confirming that he must
have recognised me, or at least Sadie, from the beach as
much – well, not quite as much – as I'd recognised him.

'Thank you and the best of luck to you and your lovely
bride,' I responded, 'but I have to get up to the train station
to pick up a mate from America.'

'We'll see the both of you then, when yous get back,' the
freshly minted groom said as he was being moved on a sea
of people through the pub's small door. 'We'll be at this for
a while. At least …'

I couldn't make out if he continued the thought, and a
second sentence, with how long they might 'be at this' or if
it was all one thought: '…for a while, at least'. Either way, I
knew where Joe and I would be having his first pint in The
Town – hell, maybe even on our way back from the station
in The Larger Town.

Chef Joe arrived the day before Christmas Eve, and
the Trinkets found The Town via their own hired car later
that same night. That the couple was driving from Dublin
was the reason we had to excuse ourselves from the post-
wedding festivities as early as we did. Like so much in my
life, the circumstances of the occasion gave the appearance
of a much larger involvement by me than was actually the
case.

'Jesus, Trevis!' exclaimed my Guinness-laced friend.
'You've been here, what, SIX WEEKS? And you're
already getting invited to fucking weddings?' His actual

pronunciation was a slightly slurred 'gedinnvitedtooo', but I got the point.

Rather than explain the whole story, from post-stag night naked swim to the footpath invitation, I simply raised my upturned palms, shoulders and eyebrows in unison – international guy's sign language for 'What can I say?' – and left it at that.

I had not slipped into total professional oblivion when I stopped working, and Chef Joe was one of the people who made sure of that. Along with a few other chef colleagues from my last company and associates who became friends, I was eventually kept in the loop enough to feel a semblance of self-worth. Management didn't seem to want anything to do with me, as if I had some control over my need to retire. Coworkers, however, started to call, request support and even ask for a bit of consulting from time to time.

These little gigs were never about the money, though living on disability insurance with expensive health-insurance premiums, spousal support and mounting medical expenses eroded my slight savings like the poorly constructed levee that it was. They were more about being a part of something. When Beth and I moved in together, it went a long way toward suturing my emotional wounds, but she was in the throes of opening a new concept high school in Seattle. Her involvement in and enthusiasm for her chosen profession was beautiful to see in someone else, but a stark reminder of my concurrent self-exile and professional abandonment.

Eventually, even the little speeches, lectures and simple consultations became more of a physical and cognitive burden than I could carry. That I could eventually recognise this for myself and then communicate the same was a major step for this former work addict. The real friends – far too many to mention, really – from my former life, such as Joe, helped me more than they'll ever know. Somehow, though, I was becoming less and less connected. The connections I was able to maintain became not only more important but also stronger. 'Fuckin' Trevis ...' was Joe's response. 'Some things never change and some people just keep gettin' better ... and then, there's Fuckin' Trevis!' These words, along with back-slapping and plenty of laughter, propelled us into several blocks worth of reminiscing as we headed to the pub where I'd told the Trinkets to meet us. It was easy to find The Cottage if you knew where you were going. If not, the local watering hole, which sat at the corner of the coast road and the main turn into The Town, made for an ideal meet-up location. And it was owned by a neighbour I'd recently discovered. That Joe and I had our snoots full and I'd graduated to a forearm crutch in the last few days made the lift the Trinkets could offer us a required one.

22

The Christmas Week

THE SUN SET BEHIND the coastal hills of Kerry just before 5 p.m. on Christmas Eve, and we all set ourselves to decorating The Cottage with the little bit of festivity we had on hand. The old, repurposed linen press in the sitting room held a revolving Christmas tree of about twelve inches, though the mechanism that caused the intended revolving seemed to have taken the night off for religious reasons. Also stuffed into the back of the old cupboard was an electric candolier holding five plastic candles and bulbs, four of which worked.

I'd bargained with a young man of fifteen or sixteen at The Town's outdoor Christmas bazaar for a length of holly that he sold me from a haystack-sized pile behind his knife-and-saw-adorned table. An old and dusty glass vase was about the only other helpful decoration found in the press. Cleaned as best we could, it held our holly in the front window and we draped the branch with a long tartan ribbon from a gift box sent to me from my auntie in Missouri.

That the box, along with my other mail, was being sent to me in The Town cemented this as an actual 'move', by my definition. When on Temporary Assigned Duty in the

Coast Guard, my mail was never *sent* to my new address, only forwarded. Permanent Change of Station, even for a short period of time, entailed a change of address and thus a 'move'. I kept this definition in my civilian life. It was for that reason that I say that I 'lived' in Ukraine, even though my stay as an ambassador for the US Agency for International Development was a temporary one. A few letters were sent to me at the agency's headquarters in Kiev and made their way to the villages of my far-off assignment. Getting letters, cards and packages from Postman Pat in The Town made me feel a little less like a poser and slightly more like a resident.

We placed whatever cards and gifts we had to exchange for the holiday under our Christmas branch, and I began preparations for our dinner. Mr Trinket made the comment that having venison on Christmas Eve was akin – obvious connection to the holidays and all – to having rabbit on Easter. Not unheard of among my friends. The previous Easter, in fact, a chef friend of Italian descent had me over for a most pleasing braised hare and hand-rolled pappardelle pasta dinner.

I barded our exceptionally lean roast with slices of lardo, an Italian fatback, cured with salt and herbs, that I'd smuggled into the country in my checked baggage. My friend Armandino back in Seattle was one of the first in America to bring this near-forgotten form of salume to the country. As I covered the purple-red meat around the deer's spine with thin slices of alabaster contraband, I had to laugh at myself a little bit. I'd no issue with concealing prohibited pork products in my travel case for culinary effect while I wouldn't even have considered bringing a small pinch of herbage that would have relieved the MS symptom that emitted from my spine at nearly the same spot where this roast had been cut from the deer.

Our 'Rudolph Roast,' as Mr Trinket had taken to calling it, was served alongside buttery colcannon flecked with as much green from kale as it was white with floury potatoes, and sauce made from wholegrain mustard and rich port wine. It made for a memorable dinner as well as an appropriate base for our evening's frivolity down the pubs.

Like no other time or place with which I am familiar, Christmas Eve endeared The Town to me forever. The courteous bustle of the days leading up to and including Christmas Eve had been supplanted with the 'goodwill toward man' of which Luke wrote and that Linus so artfully extolled in 'It's Christmas, Charlie Brown', a staple of the Christmases of my American youth. Friends embraced and visitors became friends on street corners and in public houses. Publicans bought a round or two for loyal patrons while music lightened both air and feet.

Mothers danced with sons, husbands with neighbours, and wives with one another in an air of celebration that brought the magic of the season from deep within my memory to the present, and they were nothing like the joys of this night. Children were dazzled by the fairy lights strung from one end of the ceiling to the other. That was one difference for sure – children in the pubs. Growing up where and when I did, the very thought of a child in a bar would get a business shuttered faster than over-serving a judge's wife. Here, the communal living room held every generation of the town and likely even the judge and his wife.

As the eve progressed there was a palpable increase in excitement and expectation, as if the appearance of Father

Christmas himself was imminent. The pace of the evening progressed as a reel progresses to a jig, from quarter-time to compound meter. Even the intake rate of pints and soft drinks seemed to quicken as the parties progressed. Moments before the evening felt headed for launch from its pinning, however, the elderly women of the crowd paid scurried attention to their watches.

With knowing nods and the hurried gathering of layers of outer clothes, the crowd thinned like a deciduous forest in an October windstorm. Though the pub was full when the evening began, fewer than half the patrons were left when the band finished its final song, and the lights brightened the room as if the star of Bethlehem had descended.

The 'Drinking-Up Hour' is normally a firm event in Kerry public houses but can often be extended on holidays. I guess I'd expected a little laxity on this eve of such communal celebration. Once we stepped out into the cold and clear night, I understood the abrupt end to the evening's excess. To a person, the patrons pouring from the brightly lit doorways on the main street moved in one direction up the street. No one headed for cars or home, nor did they sneak to the one pub in town where the clock was set back fifteen minutes in order to stay open a quarter hour later, thus offering the homeward bound one last swallow before saying 'goodnight'.

The pubs had to close early enough for the patrons of The Town to make it to Christmas Eve Midnight Mass at one of the two churches whose steeples pointed skyward. Though the buildings were only a few hundred yards from one another, the congregants of The Town exhibited none of the Protestant and Catholic angst palpable in towns I'd visited in the North. They wished one another 'Happy

Christmas' as they peeled one way or another in front of the two formidable buildings.

I felt like a salmon that hadn't gotten the word when I turned toward the faces of revellers swimming upstream to become pilgrims.

Joe and the Trinkets decided to take in services at the Catholic Church. I, on the other hand, decided on a long, cold walk, forearm crutches and all, back to The Cottage alone. Not that the warmth and multifaceted comfort of a Christmas Eve service didn't sound appealing to part of my brain. To my heart, though, the idea was painful.

My faith in the God I had grown up believing in was lost on a cold October day in upstate New York when a dear friend and two of her children, out for a walk on a beautiful autumn afternoon and only a few yards from their home, were senselessly run down by an inattentive driver and killed. Though I still go into Catholic churches in cities I've visited in other countries to light a candle for my Da's dear, departed mother, I do it in her memory and only out of respect for her faith. I do not believe that the accumulation of a United Nations worth of candles would elevate her soul from purgatory into heaven, but I wish I did. In a mountainside Orthodox Church of the Russian tradition in Ukraine, at the holy site of Knock in County Mayo and in quiet places of meditation spanning many Eastern religions, I have searched but have always left the same way: my head acknowledging that there is nothing there for me and my heart achingly wishing there were.

My wrestling match with religion is not over and I have no idea how it will end. But I did not intend for this evening to finish with me in a church pew, reciting prayers and hymns that I still knew by rote and feeling like I was missing something. I intended to make my way up the hill and sit quietly by a fire with Sadie and enjoy a dram of what I could understand rather than beat myself up for what I wanted to believe in but could not.

At the corner of Main Street and the road up to The Cottage, I was surprised by a very Christian act of kindness. Mrs Trinket understood a little bit of my struggles with religion, for we'd had conversations on the topic in the past; she also lives with MS. She and Mr Trinket swung their hired car to the kerb and drove me home before returning for Midnight Mass.

* * *

The week in between Christmas and the New Year was significantly mellower than I had anticipated. Christmas Day, for example, included some cooking – the most exquisite goose I'd ever laid my hands to, if you were wondering. There was also some driving about the countryside, general relaxation and a romp on a remote strand for Sadie, the day being so very warm and sunny for the season. A game or two on the cribbage board that Nigel and Joan had left occupied us all at various times in the evening. Mr and Mrs Trinket planned out day trips and a couple of overnight excursions.

Mr Trinket would only stay into the first week of January while Mrs Trinket, retired due to her MS, was slated to be with me another two weeks beyond his return. They wanted to get the most out of the romance of the small towns and villages of Kerry. The thin walls and cramped sleeping arrangements would offer little in the way of private romantic moments, even with the doors closed.

Sentinel Sadie.

Like Nigel and Joan before them, the Trinkets had to rely on quick, 'Oh, I forgot my …' or 'We'll meet you back at The Cottage' interludes if they wanted any alone time.

Joe, Sadie and I filled the week with stops at the pubs of The Town and its surrounds. Often it would simply be a pot of tea we'd share, as neither of us wanted to have to deal with the difficulties of driving the thin and winding country roads with anything to slow our responses. I found driving difficult enough in Ireland without slowed reactions compounding my situation. Like the construction of a good pint of black, the time it takes to arrange for a cup of tea allows for the cordialities of a time that, in America at least, has been replaced by 'quick-served' whatever.

We also spent some time at the hiking equivalent of 'car camping', where we would look for more of my wonderful Ps on the map and find out why someone would put a car park at the end of a road or in the middle of nowhere. Sadie was still on a three-times-a-day feeding schedule, so we'd bring a lunch with us as we headed out after breakfast – hers and ours. The places where we stopped for Herself's midday feedings were some of the most stunning vistas either Joe or I had ever seen. At cliffs and strands, on hillsides and in meadows, I would make Sadie's meal by taking her flexible cloth bowl from one coat pocket, a baggie of her food from another and a bottle of water from yet a third.

The photographs we took of the scenes could have filled a brochure of potential real estate sites for chefs whose restaurants would be challenged to create cuisine to match the breathtaking vistas where my Wheaten Terrier scarfed down kibble from a neoprene dish. She was, and still is, a photogenic little girl. Though my photographic skills are restricted to the binary combination of 1) Aim and 2) Shoot, the digital images that would fill my laptop's screen every night when they were uploaded never failed to make me catch my breath, even though I'd been the one to take them.

I was quite surprised to see a number of my photographs accompanying the article I'd written about adopting Herself in the aforementioned regional magazine. I'd sent a few of my snaps to the editors along with the piece so they might get to know the Sadie about whom I was writing. 'Sentinel Sadie' atop a stone wall and intently watching a herd of milk cows; 'Kiss-ass Sadie' nose to nose (actually touching)

Kiss-Ass Sadie.

with a donkey as they greeted each other through a wire fence; and my favourite, 'Contented Sadie' with chin-on-paws-on chair arm looking down on my camera lens after what must have been a tiring encounter with the farm animals of Kerry. All would end up in print and the sight of them was a pleasing surprise.

Sadie also showed up as something of an Internet sensation within the MS world that week. I wrote and hosted monthly webcasts for the online health company EverydayHealth.com, which interviewed healthcare professionals about aspects of living with MS. The company

Contented Sadie.

took some of the photos I'd been emailing to a few friends and colleagues back in America and made them into a slideshow. These were overlaid with a telephone interview they'd recorded, with me standing in the now infamous 'Billy's Phone Box' as pre-Christmas traffic rumbled by, and posted on their website. The feature can still be viewed today. It wasn't the last time this same phone box would play a role in my stay.

🍃 🍃 🍃

There was one photo, and the comment Da had made about the shot, which was haunting me.

On the morning of our joint, if staggered, departure from The Cottage to the train station in The Other Larger Town, I was able to capture a rainbow in a particularly wonderful picture. The arched spectrum can regularly be seen around these parts of Ireland – where the land meets the sea and they all reach for the sky. This curve of colour started a few hundred yards on the other side of the laneway in front of The Cottage, as a small squall came down the hillock from the east.

As the misty cloud slipped down toward the lane and thus The Cottage, the air around it became a muted haze, and it grew fainter in colour. The cloud entered my front garden, the sun was completely dulled for a brief moment and with it came the dancing colours of the bow. I knew this sensation of being within the rainbow from a like squall which passed my ship, or rather into which the USCGC *Yocona* entered, when transiting the long track line I'd drawn from Kodiak Island, Alaska, to the northwest tip of Oahu Island, Hawaii.

On that day, flying fish skipped over the cat's-paw waves, and not a few landed on deck where our Filipino cooks quickly gathered them for an impromptu addition to the evening's meal.

Having seen the vivid colours of the bow through the kitchen window, I opened the top half of The Cottage's Dutch door and called the others. We were all soon out in the garden. As I stood there, no piscine offerings scurried about, but the resident sheep acted much more disturbed than I'd seen them in the rains and mists that occupied at least some part of nearly every day in The Town.

I quickly made my way around The Cottage as the rest of our party made for the door. 'Back door! Back door!' I cried out as I limped around the stone building, using its knobbed walls to support me.

They soon joined me on The Cottage's advertised 'spacious back patio with furniture and a barbecue'. Spacious, indeed … There wasn't room for the rickety excuse for a picnic table let alone the five adults who tried to crowd the space.

I was alone, though, at the moment when the air once again brightened enough to make the grey lighten to blue and that blue spread into the full range of visible colour. The colours intensified as the cloud moved down the back garden and into the valley. The rest knew that the rainbow had passed through us, and there was something of an uncomfortable shudder about each of us in the understanding. As it grew brighter with every yard and each moment, so too did our collective disposition. We felt washed and freshened like the air the drizzle had cleaned.

Da was holding my camera in his dominant left hand. He'd had the forethought to grab it from the table. Or perhaps, in a way Da has always been able to do, he'd recognised something special was going to happen by the singular tone in my voice as I shouted orders for our crew to head astern. Taking the camera from him, I wall-walked myself to the corner of the house where the view of the coloured cloud's path up the other side of the valley was clear of the garden's unkempt hedges.

It was from that spot, leaning on the cold stone of the morning-shaded side of the building, that I zoomed and snapped several photos of the colours. You never really know what your exposures will look like, even with immediately gratifying digital cameras. I did, however, feel an excitement at what I might have captured. So, while everyone else was readying themselves for our relay race to the train, I booted up my laptop, plugged the two devices together, and downloaded my quarry. I clicked through the dozen or so images as they slide-showed themselves on my screen.

My breath caught when the next to last picture revealed itself to me. By this time, Da had somehow descended the stairs and now stood across the room behind me.

'You know what you have to do with that, don't you?' he said in an almost reverent voice. He must have felt the same marvel that I've heard people who have witnessed a total solar eclipse experience and forever revel in. The awe of our spectral contact.

'What?' I almost whispered in reply, feeling another strand of attachment in our adult bond.

'Well,' he stated, in an ever stronger tone of assurance, the way his voice used to grow in strength and volume as we walked from a family graveside on a particular relative's birthday, 'if someone took a picture of my house, sitting inside of a rainbow, I think I'd like to have it. Wouldn't you?'

Of course I would want to have a framed capturing of this event if I lived in the tidy white farmhouse on the other side of what I was coming to think of as my valley. I believe that it was in that very moment that I came to understand what I'm pretty sure my father knew as soon as he saw me interacting with the butchers at Mr Sheehy's shop.

'I've never seen you more at home, Son,' he said.

Da didn't call me 'Son', not ever … not because he wasn't proud to be my father and I his son. Rather, I think, it was because he never felt the need to make 'fatherly statements' such as that. It certainly wasn't because he didn't have fatherly wisdom to pass along: he had that in spades. I learned the things a man should learn from his father by watching how he lived, not by listening to what he said. Again, not that he didn't say some pretty profound – and some damned funny – things. Whatever 'Son' was intended to mean, hearing it had its intended effect. I heard the sentence over the next month … and still do.

I'm pretty sure he wanted to convey the weight of his conviction. Also, Da had travelled to stay with me in nearly all the cities I'd lived in. He had seen me in all but a few of my local environments. That The Town was where he saw me living was exactly what I finally saw as I looked at the barns and outbuildings of the white house. They were all their natural colour, while the white of the residential building on the property was swiped with nature's paintbrush by the rainbow that had enveloped and then passed The Cottage and all of us.

Red, orange, and yellow streaked the house from its upper left corner to where the hedges met the lower right. Just a hint of blue touched the lowermost part of the garden on the property's right side.

It was as I delighted in the colours of the rain on the old house that I felt them first sweep through and then swell inside of myself. I *would* make sure the family who lived two thirds of the way back up the other side of my valley got a print of the photograph, and I *knew* that my three-month stay would not quell my 28-year desire to live in Ireland for a while. A while would not be enough.

The first step I had to take in making Da's prophecy come true would be getting this bucolic tableau into the hands of the farm's inhabitants. Only then could I think of actually

Inside the rainbow.

moving my American life to The Town permanently. This was the reason I was haunted by the photo, and after another month in Kerry, it made me feel more adamant that The Town might indeed be the place for me. I had no way of knowing that it would be another six years before I would actually move, almost six years to the date, nor did I have even the slightest inkling of the direction my life would take in that time. The sense was stirring, though, the way a hunger for a turkey sandwich in the evening stirs in your mind while dining on Thanksgiving dinner.

I was only finishing my second course and already I was thinking of my next meal.

23

On Into the New Year

THE OLD YEAR, and thus the first two-thirds of my stay, was set to end in the way years always ended in The Town. Fireworks would light the harbour sky, pub-goers would empty into the streets, and the collective musical ensembles from those same public houses would play all five verses and five choruses of Auld Lang Syne while the gathered masses sang and re-sang the first one or two.

Our final meal of the year was a simple honey-roasted duck with creamed Brussels sprouts and black pepper spaetzle. The single but meaty duck proved to be plenty for all of us to eat even though the Trinkets had returned from their week of B&B-hosted shagging. The richness of the duck coupled with the heft of the German dumplings lay what I hoped to be substantial footing for what was expected to be a night on the beer.

I felt pretty special to have been invited to The Neighbour's pub on the occasion of meeting him in town a few days earlier. We four descended the hill while Joe was enthusiastically relating the 'Fucking Trevis' stories, in relation to the neighbourly summons, to the Trinkets. They'd returned to find themselves shifted from what I only now understood to be the 'warm' end of the house and their former bedroom to the room I'd occupied for nearly two months. I'd grown accustomed to the singular white radiator in my room and the short stack of inadequate blankets for warmth. I'd had two months to acclimate. Mr Trinket had only a few days before he would leave and they (and then Mrs Trinket, alone) were slated for 'my' room until a few days after his departure.

The blush of our new-found local importance washed from all our faces upon walking into the pub by the back door. There was a total lack of movable space from the rear door to the front – including the all-important route from anywhere in the room to the bar. Apparently an 'invitation' to the event was something of an open affair – open to most of the county, it would seem. The scent of scores of brands of ladies' perfumes was matched by the apparent three varieties of men's musk available in the local chemist's shop. The din of the room could actually be felt on the skin as the air pulsed with laughter and swayed with song.

The musicians, many of them surprisingly young, were banished to a preciously small space against the wall farthest from the workings of the taps behind the old wooden bar. There was no fear for their well-being, however, as an overhead bucket brigade skilfully passed a constant supply of pints and soft drinks from one end of the room to the other. I was honestly feeling like I might have let my guests down with our proffered 'invitation' to what I thought was to be a more private gathering. The combined infusion of excited surprise along with hearing my name shouted from behind the bar put those fears to rest.

'FÁILTE, Trevis! *Céad míle fáilte!*' The Neighbour shouted as he waved first at me and then to a freshly started bucket brigade of four darkened pint glasses making their hand-over-hand way in our direction.

'Ye are very welcomed!' he yelled as the beers dropped into our hands as if they were glasses of manna from an Irish heaven. 'On the house! Happy New Year!'

There would be little doubt of surviving on this thick – and surely nutritious – liquid for forty years, to be sure. Living in this room of combined body heat for that long would be unthinkable. We were jostled farther from the rear egress with every opening and closing that ushered in new invitees. Luckily, each time the back door was opened, a rush of cold, fresh air streaked in the propped-open front entrance. It swirled about the crowded room and was flushed out the back hallway like a huge, atmospheric toilet.

We shed our layers as beads of duck-fat sweat dampened our foreheads. We drank deeply of our pints and were embraced both literally and figuratively by the party and its attendees. The rare treasure of an empty stool was transported to both Mrs Trinket and me upon the collective recognition that we were both relying on walking sticks for our limited ambulation. As a matter of fact, I don't think a dead man would have made it to the floor for the human density of the space. The kindness of others is not one to be taken for granted, however, and sitting or standing, there was little moving about the room to be done anyway.

We raised our glasses to the health of our host and drank of them deeply. Placed as we were with the vastness of the gathering between us and the bar, there was concern that we might not be able to replenish when those four were drained. It was then that I noticed cash and pints being handed to and from the bar, not unlike what I've seen and been a part of as countless frankfurter brigades make their way down a seating row at American baseball games.

One simply got as close as one could to the crush at the rail and gestured to the attentive barmen. Fingers raised on the part of the patron indicated the number of pints, followed by a point in the direction of the particular 'flavour' of each requested glassful. The responding fingers represented your charge. Up the crowd, bills and coin were passed; back came change. A few minutes later – time during which conversation would ensue with whomever you might be standing near – the glasses were passed from bar to the awaiting purchaser.

It was a new system to all of us, but judging by its efficiency and cordiality, I'd have to guess that it was standard holiday practice in The Town.

Songs broke out spontaneously – solos, duets, trios and larger ensembles – from all over the room, like folksong whack-a-moles, in-between songs and sets by the band. One group of older gentlemen very near our outpost overtook the attempts of a solitary balladeer on the opposite side of the pub's Christmas tree from us. The famous Seán Ó Sé tune, 'An Poc ar Buile', about an 'Old Puck Goat' was their offering. Feeling the evening, not to mention the pints, and having accompanied many a version while driving with Sadie over the previous months, I joined in the chorus … in Irish!

Their circle of five men opened and moved close enough that the oldest of the quintet could put his arm around my shoulder. Not much movement was required, which was lucky because the lack of mobility in the room would have given any fire marshal an aneurysm. We all leaned in together with our chins toward the ceiling and uttered a joint howl …

'*Alliliú puilliliu, alliliú tá an poc ar buile. Tááááááááááá an poc ar buile!*' we sang at the top of our surprisingly harmonic lungs.

In the lyric, the mad old goat chases the narrator all around the countryside. Unbeknownst to me, until I was told by Your Man with his arm around me, the song references his abode, which is not far from The Town. I was complimented on my Irish, which I assure you was merely phonetic. I had always sung it as 'Alaluh willaluh, alaluh ahhhhhhh, en pocker willa.' The Trinkets and Joe just shook their heads, and I saw the latter smile and mouth the words, 'Fucking Trevis!'

🖋 🖋 🖋

Arms around one another, the entirety of the town sang in the streets when the clock on the Garda station clicked over to midnight. It must be remembered that The Town hasn't even a traffic light, let alone a clock tower. Below the blue stained-glass lamp, emblazoned with the symbol of the Garda Síochána, was a modest, double-sided clock. The front was visible up and down the street. The two faces of the timepiece rarely announced the exact same time. I half expected the north half of town to celebrate the New Year a few minutes before or after our side, but the sergeant must have tasked an officer earlier in the day to synchronise them and undo the Celtic time rift caused by the Christmas loudspeakers on the main street.

Kisses at midnight have to be the reason relationships begin where they should not and linger beyond their use-by date. No one, no matter how communal the celebration, wants to be without someone to snog at the passing of the year. Sure, polite and sometimes mildly impolite kisses are passed between complete strangers at 00:00:01, but a long, wet and appreciated pairing of lips is what you really want on 31 December.

Mr and Mrs Trinket revelled in theirs, as did many of the townsfolk. Joe and I exchanged the knowing glance of the recently single and made our way back into the pub ahead of the masses, still attached at their lips. Some of the older patrons were also heading in out of the cold as were a number of The Town's ardent, if somewhat reluctant, bachelors. Waiting for our drinks, I reminded Joe that there were three single women a couple of time zones to the west and several thousand feet in the air who would soon be celebrating the New Year and in fewer than twelve hours joining us for breakfast in The Cottage. It was easy to get a pint as the crowd lingered into the night. So easy, in fact, that we may have gotten a bit ahead of ourselves. In the time it took us to discuss his chances with the incoming prospects, the crowd thickened again. We crossed from hydrated to pissed and decided that a taxi would be our best option. Near the snug we found the Trinkets chatting up another lovely couple and informed them that they were on their own.

We made our way into the place where the night before becomes the morning after and on into the New Year – alone, but hopeful.

Representing the USA at a cookery demonstration in Bavaria, Germany, in 1999.

PART V
The Journey Continues: Supper Recipes

24

Supper Recipes

MANY A LIP WAS UPTURNED and eyebrow cocked when my friends on the culinary periphery heard that I was to spend the winter in Ireland. Those in the know, however, smiled and nodded their approval. As a geologic member of the British Isles, Ireland is unfairly disrespected by many Americans when it comes to cuisine. Irish food is often lumped into the 'boiled meat' camp of 1930s English cooking lore. The fact of the matter is that the food products – meat, fish, vegetables and the like – of Ireland (and the west of Kerry, in particular) have become renowned the world over.

One source of the long overdue attention was the return of many Irish citizens to the island during the days of the Celtic Tiger economy. With money in their pockets and tastes refined around the world, returning expats demanded more of their food and local chefs, who'd known all along that they had amazing raw materials. These chefs redefined 'Irish Cooking' as something old, something new, something borrowed and something very, very Irish.

I had no intention of trying to create some Irish-American Fusion Cuisine on the four burners and small cooker of The Cottage. Rather, I used indigenous ingredients and classic cooking methods to turn out hearty and tasty

Trevis, the then Operations Director of the California Culinary Academy, with lead instructor Chef Mial Parker, having a bit of fun during a photo shoot in 1998.

country meals for myself and my guests. One of the most popular meals – Steak & Guinness Stew, Colcannon and Roasted Root Vegetables – I offer to you in this section. We dished it up served together not only in the same meal but in the same bowl or on the same plate. Feel free, however, to use the sides on completely separate occasions.

This is not like the vegetable-laden stews I grew up eating. Rather, this is just meat and a few aromatics braised in a flavourful liquid. The stout in the broth can be a bit bitter without the addition of sweetness in the form of roasted vegetables as an appropriate foil. Colcannon – I like to use kale in my colcannon, rather than cabbage – lends both creaminess and weight to the dish.

Please feel free to play around with the recipes, but only after you've made them by closely following the instructions at least once. They are the result and combination of several oral versions repeated to me by cooks and housewives who don't use a recipe for something as core to their being as these basics are to the Irish country kitchen.

While the dish is stated to yield a meal for four, an extra potato or two and a few extra carrots will stretch the meal for the unexpected guests who will be knocking at (or down) your door when they hear what you're serving.

—Steak & Guinness Stew —

Serves 4

30ml/2 tablespoons vegetable oil

30g/1 oz/2 tablespoons butter

1kg/2 lb beef chuck cut into 4 cm/1½ inch cubes and patted dry

Salt & black pepper

1 large onion, peeled and thinly sliced

1 sprig fresh thyme

4 leaves fresh sage

2 bay leaves (one if fresh)

4 sprigs parsley

30g/1 oz/¼ cup flour

330ml/12fl oz/12 oz Guinness Stout

700–800ml/1–1½ pints/3–3½ cups beef stock (or good quality canned broth)

Method

Preheat oven to 180°C/350°F/Gas 4.

Heat an ovenproof casserole on med–high heat and melt 1 tablespoon butter in 1 tablespoon oil until the foaming subsides.

Divide meat into two (or even three) batches.

Salt and pepper ONLY the batch about to be browned.

Place meat in a single layer – with plenty of space between cubes – in hot fat and DO NOT MOVE for at least 4 minutes to brown.

Stir and continue searing until beef is well browned; remove to a plate.

Repeat with remaining fat and meat in batches, turning the heat down if the brown bits on the bottom of the casserole begin to darken too much.

After removing the last of the meat, turn down to medium, stir in onions and herbs (tied with kitchen twine for easy removal later). Cover for 2 minutes, remove cover and stir.

Cover for an additional 2 minutes (4 minutes total).

Stir in flour to create a pan roux – it may stick to the pan a bit – and cook for 3 to 4 minutes.

Slowly stir in Guinness, scraping the brown bits up as you stir.

Add beef with its accumulated juices and stir.

Stir in beef stock and bring to a hard simmer but not a boil.

Cover with lid and place into oven and turn down to 140°C/275°F/Gas 1 for 2–2½ hours, until meat is tender.

Take bouquet garni from the stew and discard. Return stew to oven, cook uncovered for 30 minutes to reduce and darken the stew.

Serve topped with colcannon and roasted root vegetables.

—*Colcannon*—

Serves 4

700g/1½ lb russet (baking) potatoes, peeled and quartered

450g/1 lb kale, washed, stalks removed and chopped medium coarse

150ml/5 fl oz/⅔ cup cream

50g/2 oz/¼ cup butter

1 bunch scallions, cleaned and sliced

Salt & black pepper to taste

Method

Place potatoes in a large pot with enough cold, salted water to cover by about 8 cm/3 inches.

Bring potatoes to a boil and reduce heat to a slight simmer until nearly tender, about 10 minutes.

When potatoes are still about 5 minutes from being tender, add kale to the water and stir, being careful not to break potatoes.

At that point, add cream, butter, scallions, salt & pepper to a small pan and bring to a simmer (do not let this mixture boil).

When potatoes are tender, drain and shake well. Return pot to low heat to dry and place potatoes with kale in the warm pot for 2 minutes.

Mash potatoes and kale until there are no potato lumps.

Stir in cream/butter/scallion mixture a bit at a time and fold in with a wooden spoon until at the desired consistency.

Correct seasoning with salt and pepper. Serve hot over stew or as a side dish.

—Roasted Root Vegetables—

Serves 4 to 6

350g/¾ lb carrots, peeled

350g/¾ lb parsnips, peeled

350g/¾ lb turnips (purple-topped), peeled

350g/¾ lb swede (sometimes called 'yellow turnip'), peeled

20g/½ oz/1½ tablespoons melted butter

1 tablespoon honey

1 teaspoon dry thyme

Salt & black pepper

Method

Preheat oven to 230°C/450°F/Gas 8.

Cut all vegetables into 2–2.5 cm/¾–1 inch cubes/lengths and place in a large bowl.

Melt butter with honey and thyme.

Toss vegetables with butter/honey mixture and season well with salt and pepper.

Transfer to a roasting dish and place in preheated oven.

Reduce oven temperature to 200°C/400°F/Gas 6 and roast until tender, about 1 hour, stirring about 4 times in that hour.

If serving on top of stew, you can make stew in advance and keep it warm on the stovetop until vegetables are done.

PART VI

January

25

The Cassoulet Rule

THE BARMAN AT THE TAPS had given us the business card of The Town's taxi 'service'. The service was one single car with one driver. 'On-call 24-7' read the glossy print on said card. The more important information for us that night was not listed on the advert, but passed along with a finger alongside the nose.

'Your Man,' said the barman and leaned in to nearly whisper, so as not to be heard, 'has been off the drink for years. He'll be the one to get most of us home tonight.'

Joe, braced and brightened by the night's briskness, flushed with the realisation that he could call his sons on America's east coast and wish them a Happy New Year from The Town before they'd even changed into pyjamas. My mathematical skills had been spent making sure the barman got the proper coinage for our rounds. If Joe was convinced of the position of the big hand and the little hand at his ex-wife's house, I wasn't going to be the one to argue. We needed a phone box to call our long-sober driver anyway.

On the road from The Neighbour's pub to Main Street stood Billy's phone box. At least I was remembering it as Billy's phone box. While Joe was dialling the fistful of digits required to first access an international line then input the destination exchange followed by the sequence of numbers on the back of his phone card, I crossed the street and headed up a few buildings to rest against the most comfortable-looking garden wall. From that angle I could confirm that it was, indeed, Billy's phone box.

Just beyond, and at an angle that made it look as though the glass-and-metal box was topped by a large, yardarm-crossed white mast ready to set sail, was the crucifix of a front-yard shrine. Painted silver-white, it was almost phosphorescent in the dark of the night. If I turned my head to one side, not unlike Sadie had the night in front of the television set with the tigers, the mast became an aerial antenna. It was as if Doctor Who had decided to forgo cable and satellite TV bills for old-school reception.

Inertia, gravity and – that third physical force of nature – curiosity, kept my head and body leaning over to the point that gravity nearly won the day.

Beyond the telecommunications ship where Joe continued to enter numbers was a young couple extending their midnight snog to one of two possible ends. The he of the pair was at the upper-thigh point in raising the skirt of the she, and they were both beyond halfway extended over the top of the garden wall that separated the footpath from the shrine. The physics of the situation seemed obvious. The couple would either tumble over the wall and become a writhing addition to the concrete Marys at the feet of the dying Jesus or adeptly balance themselves atop the wall in the oft attempted, rarely successful roadside/shrine-side New Year's coitus.

It was a third, unforeseen and unexpected outcome that I witnessed.

The lad's hand seemed to quickly dart up the girl's leg and for a brief moment, briefs were visible. I could not tell by the young lady's reaction if the clumsy move was acceptable, but his hand's retreat, with elastic waistband in tow, was assuredly not the move to make. The 'crack' of her open palm across his face straightened me from across the road and sounded as if the sails of Joe's single-masted phone box had bit into a gale. The young man recoiled and struggled to keep himself upright in the manner I myself had returned to many a quarterdeck. He had enough in him to bolster his amorous courage but not so much as to turn the staggering blow into a knockout punch.

The girl, it appeared as she rose from her mostly prone position to standing, was quite sober relative to the teetering lad. It was now that I could see what appeared to be quite a difference in the two. Even from this distance, she seemed superior to him. In height, dress, acuity – at least compared to his apparent level of ebriety – she dwarfed the lad, and he must have known it. With only one feeble attempt at amative counter, he about-faced and made a circuitous retreat.

She then spun around and faced toward Billy's phone box. There was an authority in the way she came down strongly on her heel and a grace with which she lifted off her toes. Her gait didn't waver but the closer she progressed to where Joe appeared to be wrapping up his call, the more she began to quake above her Tropic of Cancer. The young woman was in full northern-hemisphere breakdown by the time Joe's retreat from the call put them on a collision course. He hung up the receiver and backed out of his slip without sounding three short blasts of his ship's whistle.

Joe's call with his boys must have gone well for, even at my distance, I could hear a jovial tone not perceivable in him upon his entry. He greeted the surprised girl now in his arms with the best of Boston accents.

'Happy New Yea'a!'

My friend Joe is a good man and a damned good father. His paternity must have been heightened by his freshly completed conversation with his sons and his goodness patent as Your One seemed shocked for only a moment before collapsing into his arms in a heap of sobs. Her formerly superior stature seemed childlike enveloped in Joe's arms. He seemed to swell into a big, fluffy papa bear as they stood at the edge of the halo cast by the phone box's light. They stood there – surrogate father and child – for what seemed like a long time. It may have seemed longer than it actually was because the last round had pushed the previous few to the head of my bladder's queue.

When they moved farther out of the light and leaned on a garden wall not unlike the one I'd been supporting long enough for Arthur's best to filter through my excretory system, I knew a change in my course was required.

'I'll see you in the morning, Joe,' I announced across the road's half-light.

'Goodnight, Trevis,' was his reply to me, and a softer 'Fucking Trevis' must have been for himself. Missing his sons and always a fatherly figure, Joe would surely give the girl the comfort she needed and make a mental note to remind his boys of a thing or two.

I limped back to the pub to see if The Trinkets might still be around and in any shape to drive me up the hill.

They were not, and rather to my surprise, neither were very many other patrons. Even on a holiday like the New Year, the drinking-up hour was called far earlier than I'm used to in America. Maybe the night's revellers had made a dash to fill the pub of incorrect time or maybe everyone was having more success than Your Man in front of the shrine. Whatever the reason, The Neighbour was giving final instructions to his barmen and readying himself for the temperate departure known to many a publican. He offered me a lift to The Cottage and I thankfully accepted.

The lights of The Town faded behind and below us as we drove. Somewhere in that night a drunken boy went unsatisfied, a man missing his kids acted fatherly, and three women drank in the New Year at 36,000 feet. I went to bed in the closet room and let Sadie sleep at the foot of my bed for the first time.

And so began my final month in Kerry.

*   *   *

It was on the occasion of making a New Year's Day cassoulet with dear friends in Montreal that I heard and adopted the adage, 'You can tell how the year was by how good the New Year's Cassoulet is.' I call it The Cassoulet Rule, the premise being that one uses the leftover bits and bobs from the Christmas week feasts to fortify the flageolet bean casserole from the Toulouse region of France. Traditionally some form of pork sausage and goose are used. Beyond that, I think every household and grandmother in the southern part of France has their own take on the dish.

With the quality of produce in The Town as high as it was and the number of people chipping in for the week's meals, I figured I'd make this year's cassoulet the best ever. Living out one's lifelong dream certainly made for a very 'good year', thus our New Year's Day dinner would be the best ever. That meant that we had had some serious cooking and eating to do over the holiday week. I had an extra set of trained hands in Joe, and while the Trinkets weren't chefs, they did like good food as much as any of my friends.

We had begun our gathering of 'leftovers' by roasting a bone-in saddle of local venison for Christmas Eve dinner. Roasting any meat on the bone makes for more developed flavours, a gentler transfer of heat – resulting in juicer meat – and the added benefit of leftover bones with tasty bits of meat stuck to them for making rich stock. With a saddle, the added benefit of those bones is the animal's spine. It is full of collagen that turns into gelatin when cooked with liquid and a little bit of acid in the form of wine or tomato. This gives the stock body and is one of the differences between good and great.

The 'saddle' of an animal, usually used in the culinary sense when referring to game animals – saddle of rabbit, saddle of venison, etc. – consists of the thoracic area of the spine. The meat of the loin and often, as was the case of our large roast, the tenderloin as well. This area of the animal is rather expensive, so using these bones for stock isn't very common. Most often the cervical spinal section of an animal, further up the spine and tougher than the loin, would end up in less 'refined' dishes than roasts.

Cuts from the neck (cervical spine) of lamb are often braised for stews and other preparations. Neck bones of pork are a common addition to 'Sunday gravy', which has been known to simmer on the stovetop of many an Italian grandmother. Inexpensive, with several interlacing and tough muscles, the neck is far more destined for the stockpot than bones of the loin. It's difficult for me, even as a chef, to handle this area of butchery.

This hasn't always been the case. In fact I never had the aforementioned difficulty until attending a showing of the polymerised human remains of 'Bodies, The Exhibition,' at which I saw the very area of the spine (cervical spinal vertebrae C3 & C4) where multiple sclerosis first showed itself on my MRI. I have an odd relationship to that area of the body, human or animal.

I was very surprised at my visceral reaction to the Nervous System area of the exhibit. Standing over the fully dissected central and peripheral systems, displayed in a coffin-sized glass case and suspended as if it was the only discernible part of some invisible man at a wake, I was at once fascinated, sickened and saddened. It was impossible to see exactly where, on the Invisible Man's spinal cord, my damage would lie. Around a corner, however, was the erect form of a man with its back splayed open to show the cord, encased within the vertebral foramen and resting against the cadaver's vertebral body.

I counted down from his atlas to find the very spot where my immune system had stripped the protective layer of some of the nerves that run down my spinal cord and felt an odd jumble of emotions and thoughts. Here was a perfectly healthy, albeit dead and plasticised, spinal cord taunting me while mine failed and forced me to support my body's weight with two polio-era-designed forearm crutches – which is what I required at the time. The fascination of seeing this, as if looking within my own body at the intricate simplicity of my electrical communications system, kept me staring at the man's spine in suspended time.

I turned my head this way and that, stretched my neck and tried to feel the offending plaque buried in my own vertebra. The fluid motion of my column was in stark contrast to the rigid form in front of me. He stood silent, though, while mine crunched at the area of swelling as if

I'd bitten down on the cartilaginous keel bone of a chicken's breast with every movement. The putrid grinding echoed within my skull and around my ears.

It was only years later, after trying several prescription medications, that I discovered the calming effect medical use of cannabis had on this symptom. While my state in America allowed me to fill my prescription for medical marijuana, Ireland had no such legal exceptions, and travelling the friendly skies with the otherwise illicit substance is dangerous. Lucky for me the crunching hadn't been a problem in several months. If it were to return, I'd just have to cope.

The venison spine would be one of the types of bones that would go into our pot to create a wonderful stock for our beans to cook in on New Year's Day. Also into the pot would go the carcass of a goose, sans legs, which would be turned into confit, and the bones from a duck, a rabbit and the trotter of a pig for good measure. The stock would be simmered and strained several times with the remnant bones from the night's dinner, fresh mirepoix (a mixture of half chopped onion and one quarter each chopped carrot and celery), and a bit of white wine. By the time the duck bones from our New Year's Eve dinner were strained from the pot, both Joe and I agreed that it was the best stock either of us had ever tasted, let alone made ourselves.

On New Year's morning, it was into the aroma of this amazing stock – cooking in not one but two large pans along with soaked beans, goose confit, venison sausages, smoked gammon, onion, garlic and whatever else might fit – that the final three of our holiday houseful stumbled, but I get ahead of myself.

🖋 🖋 🖋

Dogs, of course, do not have calendars. Sans calendars, our canine companions are not aware of any red-letter days announcing our intention to sleep in. It goes to reason then that I should have expected our standard wake-up time for Herself. I did not, nor did I really think about it at all until the warm ball of fur began licking me awake in the still-dark morning of New Year's Day.

I rose to find Joe snoring in the bunk next to mine, indicating that he'd wrapped up his episode of Father Knows Best at some point and found his way back to The Cottage. Sadie and I made our normal routine of it but I'll not deny it was a slower routine, and the silence of the morning was appreciated a little more. By the time Mr Trinket, the first to rise, made his descent, followed in ragged, leisurely succession by Joe and a little later by Mrs Trinket, there was as much coffee as the leaky pot could hold and a blazing fire to welcome them into the New Year.

I had also completed the prep work for a full breakfast to greet the next wave of Americans, expected to arrive within the half hour. Fresh wheaten bread was cooling and scones had been out of the oven since 7 a.m. Pans of rashers and three varieties of Mr Sheehy's sausages awaited the pre-heated cooker. Potatoes were grated and tossed with flour and longing for their go in hot duck fat as boxty. Puddings were sliced, tomatoes topped with herbed breadcrumbs, and the special treat of a dozen duck eggs stood ready to grace what would be a heavily laden table set for seven. All I would need was twenty minutes, the time I'd figured it would take for the girls to settle in and freshen up, and we would plan our day while breakfasting on mounds of traditional foods.

I'd just filled everyone's second cup of coffee (tea for Mrs Trinket) when the invasion commenced.

Cara O'Donnell, of the Donegal O'Donnells, was at the wheel as expected. Of all my visitors, Cara was the only one who'd been to Ireland before. She knew cousins who still called the far north reaches of the island home and had visited them for major family events: weddings and the occasional funeral. Cara and her oldest friend, Hester, were my landladies back in Seattle and they'd brought along Cara's friend, Loraine, who'd recently relocated to the wine country of California.

As soon as they pulled in behind the Trinkets' car, I put the pan of melted duck fat on the burner and slid the sausages into the oven. Mr Trinket took the girls up to show them their room, and oestrogen outweighed testosterone in The Cottage for the second time in as many months.

The girls looked tired when they arrived and it was no wonder. Via the combined conversations heard through the floor above and the occasional sentence or phrase shouted down the stairs, we learned of their airborne New Year's observance. After meeting up at New York's JFK airport and boarding their connecting flight to Shannon, the Terrible Treble laughed the night away with passengers and crew on their three-quarters-empty A330. I lost track of most of the rest of the accounts since focus on breakfast's timing was required. By the time I was attending the finishing touches, the house had grown oddly hushed.

'Welcome to Ireland and welcome to 2006!' I called out from the steamy kitchen. 'Breakfast is served.'

I realised that some of us might request or require a taste of the hair of the dog that had bitten us so I reached into the cupboard for the 'good' bottle to put on our well-laid table.

'How many glasses do we need?' I asked while in the cupboard.

'The question is, "how many plates do we need," Chef,' said Mr Trinket. 'The girls are all asleep. They said they were more tired than hungry and would see us at lunch.'

There are two schools of thought when it comes to beating red-eye flights, jet lag and nine-hour time differences. The one I try to follow, though the march of time and my constant travel companion, MS, makes it increasingly difficult, is to get as much sleep as possible the night before the flight, sleep as much as possible on the plane and just power through the first day for as long as practicable. At some point I catch a second wind and with any luck maybe even a third to fill my sails that first day. The second method is to take a short 'power nap' followed by a shower to trick my body and give me that extra little bit to make it into the evening and my eventual bedtime.

What people do on their holidays is, of course, their own business and I wasn't going to tell anyone, particularly my landladies, how to tackle a holiday. We four tucked into enough food for twelve. There would be plenty left over for bacon sandwiches or a sausage scramble for the freshly rested ladies to lunch upon. And Sadie got a few sausages for the New Year as well.

The girls never got themselves converted to the local time zone – not that it was a bad thing not to have seven people queuing for the bath and a half each morning.

Meals became a catch-as-catch-can sort of pell-mell affair. Breakfasts became cold buffets that could sit out or be resurrected from the fridge and augmented if weather kept us in for lunch. Dinner was often the first meal of the day for which our ladies were up in time to join. The fireplace was in near constant blaze owing to the long, nocturnal gatherings held in the living room. Our collective schedules were so askew that we might have been able to make do with one bedroom fewer and still accommodate the gathering by 'hot-racking'. Our sleep patterns seldom overlapped for longer than an hour or two each morning.

Cara, like me, felt a deep connection to Ireland and wanted to simply sit back and soak it all in. She probably came the closest to shifting her body's clock and would occasionally join us for one foray or another. Rather than hike or shop or generally sightsee, however, she simply liked to find a bench or table or stool inside, out front, or in back of just about anywhere to blend in and observe whatever scene unfolded itself for her. So relaxed but intense were her times of observation that I'm a bit surprised she wasn't the one to write a book about the trip. Evening trips down to the pubs, however, provided opportunities for us all to meet up. Because the drinking-up hour was closer to their bodies' lunchtime than bedtime, our nocturnal trio found 'after hours' clubs and even got invited to a few later night gatherings at the homes of The Town's night people. They, like The Nephew, experienced some aspects of The Town that I wasn't even aware existed. Yet another reason I expected Cara's book.

26

Lessons of Mutton and the Black and Tans

MR TRINKET WAS SCHEDULED to fly from Shannon the next afternoon. I would take Joe to his train bound for Dublin, where he would spend a couple of nights, then head to London on business before returning to the States. The Queens of the Night were to make their exodus the following day. The night before that quick cascade of departures, I planned a memorable dinner to mark our group fare-thee-well to The Town. A special order was placed with the butcher's shop, scarce but all-important 'logs' – scarce save for around the Christmas holidays in The Town – were scrounged and saved and reveille calls placed for our mid-watch standers.

In the back of one of the cooking magazines to which I'd subscribed over the years I recalled reading a French country recipe for a whole roast leg of lamb, which seemed fitting for The Cottage's equipment and former layout. What was now the living room, with its large open fireplace, had once been the kitchen of the building. 'Kitchen' in this case was really meant to speak to the end of the open floor plan where the cooking would take place. The dividing walls that now stood on this floor, and I might even guess the upstairs, had been added by The Princess and her husband when they converted the old building into the holiday rental that it now was.

Bolted deeply into one side of the open grate was a large, swinging cast-iron arm, the kind one might imagine suspending a cauldron in an old painting. The hearth of the fireplace also extended well beyond what one would consider customary for a fireplace simply expected to provide heat. Once I looked at it in this frame of mind, this was without a doubt a 'kitchen' fireplace. My plan was to use it for its original intention. Little did I know that it would give rise to such a legend that Joe's boys still ask, when he mentions that he'll be seeing me, 'You mean, the "leg of lamb in Ireland" Trevis?'

When I ordered the joint from Mr Sheehy and the lads, I had to explain not only what I wanted in the butchering of the leg, but also my intent so as to ensure their understanding of the cooking process.

'So, then ...,' said Ford, who was trying to understand my meaning, 'you want the whole crube left on, bloody hoof and all?!' sliding further into a Scottish accent with the question.

It took a trip to the Internet café and a good, lengthy search to discover that a crube on a lamb is the equivalent of a trotter on a pig – the foot.

'Not the hoof unless that's the only way you can make it work for me,' I responded. 'I only need it attached as far as the "heel" ... the ...' I searched for the right word to make my chef's intentions come across in butchery terms.

I dug back to the place in my mind where I'd stored mammalian anatomy of livestock for Meat Fabrication class in culinary school. No results. Though I dated our county's 4-H queen while a junior in high school, I was not a boy from the farm. I couldn't find the words to describe my need.

'I want to hang the leg,' I explained, 'in front of the fire … to cook it. I need to run butcher's twine between the Achilles tendon and the hock-end of the shank, so I need the attachment intact. Does that make any sense at all?' Ford cocked his head the same way Sadie would later do when I dangled the great rear quarter of the animal in what she must have considered the middle of the room. It was then that, silent up until this point in the laboured conversation, Finbar piped up from his task at the butcher's block table behind the counter.

'Has the hearth a crane?' he asked while wiping his pink hands on a white side towel, thusly transferring the colour from one to the other. 'My ma used to roast mutton legs that way when I was a boy. She hung them from a hook on the crane and turned them every once in a while so as to cook 'em evenly. Is that what you're lookin' for?'

It was the first time since our first meeting in my many visits to the shop that Finbar had actually spoken to me.

'By "crane", do you mean the iron arm that swings in front?' I asked.

'Aye,' he responded, 'has it got one of them? Is that what you're going to be hanging it from?'

'Yes. But I'm not going to use a hook. I read of using twine to loop through and then you just give it a spin,' I pantomimed, as if twisting the leg from the bottom, 'and let it turn and then un-wind and re-wind until it needs spinning again.'

'You'll not be burning any coal in the grate, now, will you? Turf'll be fine, like, but coal would ill-flavour the meat,' he warned.

I assured him that I'd saved enough 'logs' to fuel a blaze for several hours. Logs were really just split pieces of soft, round wood about ten inches long that could be purchased in sacks for Christmas fires. Never having executed this hazy memory of a recipe, I was far from sure of its success. Knowing that people have been cooking meat in front of fires for a considerable bit of time – and even into the past recent enough for Finbar to recall it – I was confident the result would be at least passable.

'I know just the one for ya,' Finbar assured me. 'He's a young wether hogget I've had my eye on for a while and he'd be the perfect bit of mutton for your plan.'

Upon protesting that it was lamb I was after and neither hog nor mutton, I got a quick lesson in the proper terminology of sheep meat. In this shop in Kerry, at least, 'lamb' is only lamb until New Year's Eve. On January first it technically becomes 'mutton', but is usually (and culinarily) referred to as 'hogget'. In many other parts of the lamb-eating world, it might be sold as lamb until it reaches one year of age and has no permanent teeth. After it reaches a year but has no more than two incisors, the meat can be called 'hogget' until that third tooth comes in, whereupon it is called 'mutton'. The word 'mutton' doesn't actually reflect the animal's age in months but the age it acquires more adult teeth. For all intents and purposes, the term 'hogget' is an older lamb that is still mild of flavour but stronger than a spring lamb, while 'mutton' is reserved for the meat of older, more strongly flavoured sheep. 'We'll have him brought to slaughter in the morning, but it'll take a good few days to get you a proper-hung leg,' Finbar said, beginning as if making a note to himself before finishing the thought directly to me.

Knowing that one particular lamb, out wandering the fields at the very moment, was to be offed for my specific meal lent a heft to my planned preparation. I had expected to just get whatever meat the lads had in the case. If the milk-toothed wether was to give his life for my fireside experiment, I was committed to doing the animal honour in his preparation. It was still a little bit odd.

Turning to Ford, Finbar directed the plan like a boatswain to an able seaman.

'Cut it between cannon bone and pastern, but do it from the front so you don't nick the tendon. Pierce a hole behind the hock so he can thread the twine.' And then, to me, he said, 'Have you twine?'

Without waiting for my answer, he was back to Ford. 'Give him a hank of twine too.' As an afterthought for which I would be quite grateful, upon carving the roast, he added, 'And take out the hip all the way to the aitch bone and tie it back in so Your Man' – it was the first time I'd been called 'Your Man' and it made me smile – 'gets the flavour, but it'll make it easier to carve. It's how Ma did it.'

And with that, Finbar was back at the butcher block. I felt it was something of a breakthrough with the Kerryman. He'd always seemed the most sceptical of this tourist trying to fit in. His hearty '*Slán*, Trevis' as I walked out of the shop along with a smiling thumbs-up through the window signalled a new level of acceptance.

With the weight of an animal's life on my shoulders as I tried to ensure the success of the dish, I spent the next few days refining my plan. First, I allowed the usually well-cleaned fireplace to build a good bed of ashes. With a well-fatted leg from a hand-chosen wether hanging in front of the fire, I expected a good amount of drippings from the process. Fresh herbs were difficult to find that time of year, but the greengrocer was able to order bunches of thyme, sage, rosemary, oregano and savory to go with the readily available parsley. I wouldn't use much herbage on the roast itself; I wanted only to accent the flavours intrinsic in the local meat, not mask them. Most of the remaining sprigs of the fragrant plants I tied and fashioned into a basting brush of sorts for the roasting.

On the morning of 6 January, I unwrapped the leg, fresh from the shop, on the countertop and rubbed it with a good bit of salt and black pepper and a couple of spoonsful of the herbs – minced, but not too fine. I then patted it with some good olive oil and pressed in a few cloves of peeled and sliced garlic. More garlic, salt and whole peppercorns went into a small pot with about a cup of the olive oil. It was into this pot that I placed my herb brush.

The roast was left to marinate and come up to room temperature for most of the day until we were ready for the culinary experiment. Next came the fire. First my reserved ash was raked from under the grate between the andirons. There was enough for a four-inch-thick bed to absorb the anticipated molten drippings. Chef Joe and I stacked pieces of round wood, picket-fence style, around the ash bed. The pile reminded me of the parade grounds of Fort Michilimackinac, at the northern tip of my home state's lower peninsula, that we used to visit annually in my childhood. Not unlike the Fort's imposing pinewood ramparts, the purpose of the barricade was to discourage attack. Rather than warding off marauding troops, however, it was the furry female of the house our rampart was intended to deter.

Ford had, indeed, pricked a perfect-sized hole in the exact place I had foreseen the twine being threaded. I fed the line through a few times to make a four-cord loop about six inches long and tied it off in smart, sailorly fashion for the vertical rotisserie.

With a good base of hot turf smouldering, Joe, who I'd put in charge of all things fire this day, began to add wood. While the heat from turf and coal was far more intense and steady, the flames from the parched coppice lit the room with bright yellow light more incandescent than the deep red radiance of our typical fuel. The first load of dry softwood quickly burned down to chunky embers, so the chef threw on a few more pieces, along with tufts of heather from the hedgerow, and I hung the leg of mutton.

We set the pot of steeped oil on one of the upturned logs nearest the fire to warm and more deeply infuse the brew.

Every two or three minutes, either Joe or I would get up from the wing-backed chairs we'd moved closer to the hearth than their normal standing places to anoint the leg with a blessing of the flavoured oil and give it a spin. I had pulled the long briar pipe, which had until this night gone unlit, and filled it with a fragrant Irish whiskey-soaked Cavendish tobacco. The room became thick with a scent spectrum of warmth.

The spicy pine fire, smouldering with lacy heather, released fat-soluble phenolics from our-meal-to-come while the smoke from my pipe's bowl added tones of vanilla from the wood that tempered the distiller's spirits.

No wake-up call was required for our vampires. The open staircase acted as an internal chimney, and their room was the first at the top of the flight. It wasn't fifteen minutes into the roasting that we heard stirring from above our heads. Within the hour they were a third of the way through their shower rotation with our hearthside tableau acting as an on-deck circle would in baseball, or a theatre's green room.

The internal temperature of our meat was taking far less time to reach the desired 50°C/130°F than I had anticipated. The thick stones of the fireplace had first absorbed and then radiated steady heat to augment the direct energy of our fire. To slow the process I simply swung the hinged crane – as I had recently understood it to be called – a few inches away from the fire. Even so, the greater-than-7 lb joint was nearing completion in just over two hours and before the last of the girls was finished in the shower.

Like the *agneau de pré-salé* of Mont St Michel Bay in Normandy, France, which has a unique flavour and texture based on its saltmarsh diet, so too does the lamb that Mr Sheehy sources have a characteristic all its own. Fragrant heather and wild herbs grow on the vast and savage hillsides where many shepherds herd their flocks for free summertime grazing. These plants root in the acidic soil and struggle their way through rock and weather to bloom in the short season. The strongly flavoured herbs counter the sweet, rich grasses of the spring and summer pastures where the lambs are born and weaned.

Sweet balances sour and light counters dark. The rich and the lean of these sheep's diet touches all of the flavour senses – sweet, salt, sour and bitter and it is magnificence. At different times since my diagnosis, I have lost two of those important building blocks of flavour. Once, for about a month, I lost the ability to taste salt. The flavours of simple,

Roasting the leg of lamb in the kitchen fireplace.

working-class street food from around the world are some of a chef's great joys. More 'innovative' dishes than you'd think are based on these wonderful flavours. I was once having a bowl of such highly flavoured but humble origin – Vietnamese noodle soup called *pho* (pronounced 'fuh' in English) – when I noted something terribly wrong in my mouth. This normally highly flavoured dish was coming across as flat and lacking. I lunch at this particular spot frequently and know the owner personally as well as professionally, so I was sure the dish had not changed. By the end of the day I had forgotten about the soup for other MS reasons, as old symptoms began to wash over me.

I had to nap four times that day and could hardly un-bed myself the next morn. The second day progressed with profound fatigue and the 'loopiness' I'd first been made aware of at my diagnosis and experienced around disease progression. I knew that something 'MS-y' was happening, and I didn't have the energy to eat, so I didn't think much about the prior day's lunch experience.

Once that phase passed, however, I noted that something was seriously wrong with this chef's palate.

While we taste all over our tongue, cheeks and the back of our throat, there are concentrations of certain tastes in certain areas of the mouth. I noted that things were heightened in some areas and absent in others. A big 'flavour hole' appeared in the centre of my tongue, where salt receptors are concentrated. I wasn't, I came to understand, tasting salt.

When trying to describe this symptom, some have said to me, 'Well, that wouldn't be too bad. I don't like salt.'

It's not just the taste of salt that goes missing when this happens to me; it becomes a spectrum of disorder. Chicken, for instance, doesn't taste like 'chicken'. Chicken tastes like a particular blend and combination of those four sensations of sweet, salt, sour and bitter. We know that combination as chicken.

I should have retorted to those downplaying my loss, 'You can't see the colour blue? No biggie, you don't like blue anyway.' But blue isn't just the colour blue. It's half of green and it's half of purple. Without blue, green is just yellow. Without salt, every flavour is wrong. The same, unfortunately, also happens to my receptors of the taste of sweet periodically and for varying lengths of time.

It's not that I care all that much for sweets, but flavours are balanced by one another. If a food doesn't have a balance (and that's not to say equal amounts) of sweet, salt, sour and bitter, we ask the eternal question, 'Does this need something?'

Think of bread or oatmeal when you forget to add that pinch of salt – yuck! Toothpaste becomes shockingly sweet, pasta tastes like its namesake – paste – and coffee is nothing but aftertaste. Potatoes taste of dirt, lovely young salads taste green and bitter like a rotting leaf off an old tree. Wine is a sour, bitter mess and beer, sans that sweet, malty grain flavour, is just a stingingly hoppy, astringent abomination.

The next time you see a colour that would be changed by taking blue out of it, you may understand a little bit of the hell this symptom can be. How would that grey, midday sky look with white clouds and yellow trees in your yard? How about a sea black as night with bright yellow seaweed shimmering in the sun? Perhaps a bunch of grapes as bright red as sour cherries in July? Or wine the colour of blood?

You would feel like your whole world was changing. That's what happens to me. The way I taste is not just a function of making my meals palatable, it is a definer of who I am. If Chef Trevis can't taste, it can feel like there isn't really a Chef Trevis any more.

My sense of taste has waxed and waned in the years since that first shocking experience, giving way to the knowledge that this neuro pathway is damaged and may one day abandon me without return. It is perhaps for that reason that I try to take conscious note of flavours both common and extraordinary. I have come to appreciate the nuances – the remarkable joys – of the simply sweet and the subtle sapor, for they will as likely end as the warm Indian summer afternoons of October. I have dined on foods great and simple, profound and homey. Ireland has

Sadie awaits her first bone.

taught me the extraordinary joy of ingenuous foods more than any experience in my professional life.

Cheap plates and mismatched flatware alongside water glasses and coffee mugs befitting the array of plonk the local supermarket availed adorned our kitchen table. Potatoes roasted in the last of my duck fat and carrots mashed with butter, cream and thyme played humble accompaniment to the headlining joint. The penny brown of our tournée-cut Kerr's Pink spuds, creamy ochre of crushed carrots and garnet slices of the late wether brought autumnal colour to the midwinter feast.

Had this unsophisticated supper been the last I was ever able to taste, the bounty from hills and fields of west Kerry would have offered the kindest of memories to accompany my bald palate. So too would have the happy sound of Sadie at her first bone, barely audible above the moans of satisfaction punctuated with laughter at the delicious absurdity of this food in this place with these people.

🪶 🪶 🪶

The pub where our septet decided to spend our final evening together was not The Neighbour's pub. Rather, we decided on a more touristy establishment that offered music nightly as opposed to The Neighbour's place, where musical entertainment was more of a whimsical happening than by design. The place had the country village pub look that the newfangled 'Irish' pubs that have sprung up around the globe have tried to emulate, at least in the décor.

'Antiques and old shit,' as Da calls it, were strewn, hung, tacked, tucked and generally displayed all about the place. There was nary a place where something could be stuck that something wasn't, from old bottles and handbills to farm implements and sports hardware. If the building couldn't support itself as a pub, curio shop was a viable second option. The surprising density of the crowd, however, put to rest any worry of its sustainability as purveyor of the drink.

Though it was a Friday night, our collective had assumed aloud, over slices of the most incredible (and with my new-found knowledge of the distinction, first) leg of mutton any of us had ever had the good fortune to devour, that the Christmas holiday season and its accompanying visitors would have made for a relatively quiet night out. What we didn't notice, and would not notice for a little while longer, was that the vast and overwhelming gender in the pub this night was female. They were older than I was accustomed to seeing in this place but were mostly, with few exceptions, women.

In the rural parts of the country the old tradition of 'Women's Christmas' is still observed on the Feast of Epiphany, and The Town is about as rural a town as you're going to find, particularly when it comes to adhering to traditions. *Nollaig na mBan* – Woman's Christmas – is one such tradition that may be dead or dying in some of the more cosmopolitan parts of the island. No one, however, had ever accused The Town or its women of being of the 'more cosmopolitan' set. In parts such as these, women are afforded a much-needed rest and night on the town after catering to the holiday needs of family and friends.

The ladies of The Town had taken off their holiday hostess' aprons and donned party attire for their well-earned evening out while the men of the family stayed at home to look after the brood. Judging by the joviality of the crowd and our difficulty finding a table to accommodate our number, many of The Town's women thought the tourist pub was the perfect setting for their end-of-Christmas do.

After a lap around the cavernous four rooms of the establishment, we found empty chairs at a table peopled by a gaggle of personable women of mixed age. Room was made, but only for the women of our group. We three lads were chased off like roosters from the chicks and sent to ferry a round for our women. Abiding men that we were, we also offered a round to the first tenants of the table. After delivering all the glasses we could carry in one and a third trips, Mr Trinket, Joe and I made for the all but empty stools at one of the four bars in the building to watch the show.

And what a show it was … most of which we were sworn to keep to ourselves by an oath of secrecy. We were 'allowed' by the ladies of Women's Christmas to stay because of two important factors: 1) we were tourists, not residents and therefore not aware of the sororital gathering we had interrupted, and likely more important, 2) we continued to purchase, if not deliver, rounds in succession.

When it was Hester's round, she came to me looking quite perplexed and in need of assistance.

Knowing that I, because of my disabilities, have inhabited a world that can teeter on the edge of political correctness, she needed advice as to the proper way to order the drink she wanted. She had been schooled in a South Boston pub she'd visited years earlier as to the inappropriateness of requesting a 'Black & Tan' in Irish pubs. The drink she referred to is a half pint of light ale topped with half pint of stout. During her apparently scarring dressing-down, she learned of the Royal Irish

Constabulary Auxiliary Force and their horrific reign over the country from 1920 to 1921.

The despicable actions of the Black and Tans touched very close to The Town and I was grateful for Hester's discreet concern.

I had no idea what the proper name for the drink might be in Ireland, never having had the desire to dilute a pint of black myself. I motioned to Your Man behind the bar and tried to order the pint as tactfully as I could.

'Your One here would like a pint of half Harp Lager and half Guinness,' I nearly whispered.

'One Black & Tan then, is it?' replied the publican.

'Right, one …' was all I could say, but Hester, who had been living for years with the fear of offending someone in ordering a damned pint of beer, wouldn't let it be.

'I thought it was offensive to call it that here,' she said with a wave of her arm to encompass the entirety of the country with her theatrical gesticulation.

Your Man behind the bar took a moment from searching for the special spoon that can be balanced on the side of the glass in order to 'float' the darker stout on top of the lighter beer.

'Look,' said Your Man, 'if we got ourselves in a bunch every time some Yank came in here and said something offensive, we'd spend more time out in the street than behind the bar.' He had a good point. 'Most of yous don't even know who the hell the Black and Tans were, let alone the shite they did. But they didn't do it to me and my family, and most of the business in this place comes from Americans anyway. You're a pretty woman. If you'd like to chat about history with me after my shift, I'm all in for it.' Hester nearly sparkled at the idea. 'We're not going to judge you for being insensitive; and I thank you for trying. But I will judge you for the felony ye'r committin' against that porter,' he said, simultaneously pointing to the glass behind him and validating my very point as to the atrocity being carried out upon Arthur Guinness's finest.

In the years that followed, I have kept the barman's thoughts in mind as I write for and speak to members of the MS community. There is such a thing as being overly sensitive when talking about this, or other conditions like mine. I'd never use the most offensive of the debilitated lexicon, of course, but I'm not going to tiptoe around on eggshells to make sure we offend no one, either. Some have gone as far as admonishing me for saying that I 'live with MS'.

'It makes it sound like that's all you do – live with the disease!' one reader once commented.

Assuredly, I never meant for my standard line of introduction at events to mean any more than 'I have it, it can't be cured, and I'm getting on with my life'. Whenever someone calls me on my relative insensitivity when it comes to disability language, I think back on Your Man and what he said. It brings things into focus … and it makes me want a pint.

27

The Rainbow Farmhouse

AS SUDDENLY AS THE holiday horde had descended upon The Cottage, they were gone – save for Mrs Trinket and her MS. I offer that in a way that only someone who knows the disease can and in a way that only someone living with it can understand and not be offended. Mrs Trinket, in this case.

I know that 'everybody's got something' and it could be said that there are far worse things than living with multiple sclerosis. But it could only be when you feel what it does to you from one day to the next, when it's your body that rebels and it is with the hands of your own systems that the thief steals from you, that you could understand. It's been said of MS that you can't 'get it' unless you get it. If that is the case, I hope that my words will never be clear enough for you to understand me completely.

So there we were, the four of us: Mrs Trinket, me and our two individual thieves. Despite my continued difficulties and that 'episode' in November, the course of my disease had been radically modified for the better by chemotherapy, while Mrs Trinket's had taken a turn for the other side since I'd last seen her in October. They say you don't really get to know someone until you travel with them. The same can be said of my ever-present companion and Mrs Trinket's too. I had learned much about my disease in the months away from my home and routine. I was learning as much about Mrs Trinket's MS as I was learning about her during her stay, and she about me and mine.

The most important lesson we learned from each other was in the freeing effect of not having to pose or try to overcome for others when it was just we two.

It was obvious to me, and is likely to you as you've read thus far, that I can act better than I am feeling and can lie through acts of both omission and commission. Again, the back of my hand is not on my forehead as I say this. We all – disease, condition, whatever-the-hell you want to call it or not – direct our own stage play of life. We reveal the parts of ourselves that we feel safe showing to our audience and cast mates and we save others only for those closest to us. Like battered actors, alone and backstage in an empty theatre, Mrs Trinket and I were forced to act for no one but each other and we chose not to act at all.

With simple, wordless acknowledgment, each of us quietly understood and accepted the other's place in the downhill slide that some medical mind had the gall to name 'progression'. We also relished the fact that we didn't have to carry around the burdensome cloaks that, even for those closest and most dear to us, are thick and heavy and serve only the purpose of shielding them from our symptoms. These garments of disguise do nothing for the person within; they only weigh us down with the responsibility of caring for others' feelings and reactions, often to our own detriment.

The two weeks alone with Mrs Trinket were at once the easiest and most difficult of my stay in The Town. There was indeed a lightness to be found in our uncostumed nakedness. The weight of the garments, once we were forced to ready ourselves and re-enter our individual stages, seemed even heavier than I had remembered them to be just those few days before.

It was during this time that I had a large print made of my photograph of the farmhouse, on the other side of 'my valley', dipped in the rainbow. At the same photo shop, tucked behind brightly coloured tourist shops, I found a lovely frame I deemed worthy of the picture. It was beautifully carved and not inexpensive, but no other seemed right for the moment my camera had captured.

Its price was not without matter, for my 'house fund' had far from kept up with expenses. The extra electricity and fuel required to keep the lights and fires burning day in and day out for the previous weeks bit deeply into what reserves the compounding car hire rates didn't consume. With around three weeks left in my stay, I had already gone beyond my budget for the trip, and an unexpected expense bounced into play via email the day after I'd purchased the frame.

On my weekly trek to the restaurant-during-tourist-season/Internet-café-in-winter to post the week's photos and update to an ever-growing address list, I was notified that my stolen car had been found by Seattle's Finest. I was required to retain a barrister in order to create and notarise an international limited power of attorney in order for my car to be released from the impound lot.

My first idea was, of course, to simply wait until I'd returned. Soon I found it increasingly difficult but necessary to call 'home' to deal with the issue. Daily storage fees at the city's impound lot would far outweigh the expense of handling the legal stuff from Ireland, but I found the whole experience disturbing in another way too. Though I'd have to part with even more money than I really had to spend, that stupid car was pulling me back to reality before I was ready to go.

My MS attack in November had robbed me of better than a week, likewise time alone with Mrs Trinket had made me face my disease (and hers) like a maggot in the custard. Now the anchor chain had paid out as far as it could and I was spun around to face my imminent return. Even with weeks before I would need to pack, my final days would be spent with my bow facing the inevitable course of my return to Seattle.

*   *   *

The road of our intentions is seldom direct, and the same can be said for most roads in Kerry. Equally, as in the long-term planning to meet goals, attain desires and reach intentions, the constant availability of either a figurative or literal road map is required. My literal map, in the form of the ever more creased and annotated Ordnance Survey, was back at The Cottage with Mrs Trinket. In the waning days of her visit she was using it to note where she and Mr Trinket had travelled and where she had snapped memorable photos. She was also listing the sights her struggles kept her from on this trip and to which she very much intended to return and experience.

Though I'd never been up the other side of my valley, the way seemed simple enough when viewed from my back garden. I even took a survey from the back windows of the first floor of The Cottage before heading out with Sadie to deliver the rainbow photo. The troubles began with several false starts up roads from the town, which I thought would lead me to the road of my eventual destination. I ended up in private drives, at pasture gates and, on one futile attempt, right back where I had pulled off the main road but facing the direction whence I'd begun.

Once I found the road to the road, the way was as clear as I'd perceived it would be and I was soon, though nearly an hour after we'd left The Cottage, at the final turn before the laneway became a muddy cul-de-sac. Sadie was very excited to see that the farm had not only dairy cows in the barn that was visible from The Cottage, but also a few sheep in a pen near the drive, chickens running all about and a large goat tied to a moveable post in the front garden. The goat and his post looked as if they were routinely moved from place to place in the garden to keep the lawn in check. Owing to this, there were no ornamental plantings in the garden. A few pots and window boxes gave the house the charm I'd expected from my far-off observations. I'd envisioned what this meeting might be like for the days leading from when I ordered the print until just now as I arrived. I envisioned being invited in for tea as the woman of the house called in the children from their play and her husband from his work in the fields. Fresh-churned buttermilk would be poured from earthen pitchers into sturdy, farmhouse mugs, and soda bread would be served warm with slices of cheese the family made from the milk of their own cows. Your Man might even ask me to sit by the fire. He'd pull out the bottle from behind the book where he'd hid it from his knowing wife. The book would sit on a shelf he'd made himself, of course.

The children would fight to sit on my lap and beg for stories of America until they fell asleep, one hand over my

Sadie who had been invited to the fireside along with their herding mutt. What I didn't envision was the reality of a relatively large – at least for The Town – working farm in mid-January.

After ringing the bell three times and hearing nothing from inside (or out) that sounded like anyone was at home, I was about to leave the plain brown sack that held the framed photograph at the threshold and drive away. Then, at the sound of my fourth and what I decided would be final ring, I heard a dog barking in the very back of the house. I backed away from the door and peered around the corner of the house to see not one but two Border collies accompanying a tall, middle-aged woman in wellies and work clothes.

I had tried to dress respectfully without looking like a missionary or travelling salesman. My corduroy trousers, turtleneck sweater, tweed jacket and cap left me overdressed but not looking like someone from the city trying to collect a debt, or at least I hoped they didn't.

When she first spoke to me I thought she was giving commands to the dogs, who responded very attentively to everything she said. I soon realised from the increasing inclination of her head toward me upon finishing a sentence that she was speaking to me, but not in a language in which I was conversational. It was familiar. She was using the Irish language, and it made me smile just a little bit that she might conclude I was a native of the area. I removed my cap in respect and realised that, while I had picked up a few words here and there in the previous months, all of the words I knew of the dialect had to do with going away and wishing someone good luck in departing.

'Hiya? Are you the woman of the house?' was all I could muster. So much for not coming across as wanting to sell her a Hoover.

'Aye. And ye?' she replied, cautiously. She must have distrusted my Fermanagh accent.

I figured it best to begin with where I was living. Where one comes from is as important as who one is in some parts of Ireland.

'My name is Trevis,' I began. 'I live in the stone cottage across the valley.' I pointed in the direction of my rental. From the back, it was nowhere near as charming as it was from the front. None of the houses on the laneway, whose backsides were visible from this angle, looked very attractive from the rear.

'Which one, then?' She had come up close to me to follow the direction of my gesture. With that I adjusted my arm to more accurately represent the compass heading of my abode.

'The stone cottage, the one just below the rain,' which was coming down from the opposite hill and about to envelop The Cottage and all of the neighbouring buildings. 'I'm from America but I've let the house from The Princess for the winter.' I added the name of the owner thinking it might help.

'Ah, you're the Yank with the Wheaten bitch from Kildare then?' Her tone didn't give away her impression of me; it simply acknowledged that she knew of me. I was at once glad that I'd chosen an Irish breed for my dog and curious as to how I might have been referred to had I not gotten Sadie.

'Aye. That's Herself in the car,' I said and gestured to where I'd left the car at the end of the drive.

I wasn't sure where to go from there, so I simply launched into what sounded more and more like a sales pitch as it continued.

'A few months ago, there was a squall that crossed the valley. It was November. My father and I were in the back garden watching the rainbow that was in the cloud as it passed. I took a couple of pictures … of the rainbow, I mean.' Then I realised I had the bag with the photo in my hand. A picture being worth a thousand words and all.

'When we looked at the photos, my Da said that I should give it to you. "If someone had a picture of my house inside a rainbow, I'd want to have it," he said. So I had it framed for ye.' I hadn't wanted to let the 'ye' slip. As I'd announced myself as being from America and feeling very much like a poser with my tweed cap in my hand, I did not want to come off as the caricature of an American in Ireland.

'Ye're sellin' it then?' she asked.

I was taken aback by her question, not only because I'd been trying to avoid the whole salesman thing, but because the thought of selling the photo had never crossed my mind.

'What? Sell? No.' I retraced and must have sounded rather juvenile, 'My Da said I should give this to you. I'm not selling it; I want to give this to you. It's your house – in a rainbow.'

'And where's your Da from?' she probed.

'His family is from Fermanagh, in the North,' I said. 'He lives in America now,' I said with a tug at the truth. 'He was over to visit me. When he saw this picture, he said I should give it to the family that lives in this house.' I pointed back and forth between the picture and her home.

'So, ye're not wantin' to sell me this. Ye want to give it to me?' She was still puzzled, but I believed she was on the path to understanding. I just needed to close the deal. I handed her the framed picture, keeping the bag in my hand, and stepped back half a pace.

'I want you to have it. It was a beautiful sight to see, your house sitting in a rainbow. My Da and I want you and your family to have this. That's all.' I continued to back away.

'I should give you some money,' she objected in a different, maybe understanding, tone. 'It really is our house,' she noticed, 'I see the rainbow.'

I didn't want to spend any more time as the salesman, poser, traveller … whatever tag she was trying to get to fit her impression of me. I just wanted her to have the picture and I wanted to be gone.

'God bless all in this house,' I said, frankly, remembering the line from the John Wayne and Maureen O'Hara film, *The Quiet Man*. 'I hope you enjoy it.' And I backed away a few more steps and punctuated the thought by putting on my cap.

She was still standing in the drive when I pulled out, looking between me, the photo and the house that the framed reproduction represented. She managed a tentative wave as Sadie and I drove away. I wished that I had just left the package at the door. Maybe she'd think the fairies had left it rather than the fat American who she thought was trying to sell her something. But then, suddenly, I was more happy that I'd come to deliver the photo and had the rather lengthy chat.

I drove the car to the side of the road and quickly got out and gazed across the valley, up beyond The Cottage to the hill that was just behind the hill across the laneway from my temporary home. I'd not seen it in the ten weeks I'd lived in The Town, but there it was, a representation of

Ireland that I'd had in my brain ever since the year after Mrs Magee had belittled my 'Irishness'.

It had been within a short walk of The Cottage the whole time.

28

My 'Happy Place'

THERE HAD BEEN A BIT of imagined Ireland that had been with me several times in my life, including the day of my diagnosis.

Just before they slide you into 'the tunnel' of a magnetic resonance imagining (MRI) tube, they fill your ears with the same memory-foam plugs used by the British military to protect soldiers when firing weaponry. First they roll the plugs between their fingers and shape them to look like golf tees. Then they slide them into the ear, where they expand to fit snugly from just behind the tragus to about an inch inside the exterior auditory canal. As the foam expands to plug the canal, the world stifles and you hear less and less until the sound of your blood in the veins of your head replaces the white noise of the room. Your breath becomes easier to focus on than the things you see in front of you, and that's fine; the next thing you see is the bars of knight-like helm being hinged over your face.

You will soon focus on the small, polished mirror that is set at such an angle that you can see your toes, and thus the window to the control room where the tech will magnetically carve the part of your body that interested your doctors enough to order the test. But first, you hear the muffled speech of the person who stuffed your ears.

They're asking you one question or another about your relative comfort, to which you answer in a voice more explosive in your head than you imagine those guns the military are protecting their ears from must sound.

Then they slide you into the tube in the same manner you've seen medical examiners push murdered bodies into coolers on crime shows, and you vow to yourself that you will stop watching CSI. Just before the clicking and whirring, the buzzing and banging begin, you are alone with your breath. You focus, for a moment, on the mirror and realise that you'd rather just close your eyes, and then you are alone. One hundred per cent alone.

It was at this position during my first MRI that I searched for a 'happy place' to go. A part of my brain needed to be quieted. The part that had run multiple kitchens in hotels, had orchestrated international financing in the former Soviet Union, the overthinking part that had begun observing, analysing, and assessing every detail of everything upon hearing that the tech would be slicing my brain and cervical spine to look for multiple sclerosis. There is such a thing as overthinking a situation. When you enter the tube for the first time, any thinking is overthinking.

With one deep Sitkari breath that I'd learned from a yoga teacher friend, I drew in a hissing breath past my teeth and tongue, then exhaled the air though my nostrils. I thought about the peaceful places we think about when we try to calm ourselves. The problem is, when we think about calming places we have been, we couple them with experiences we have had at those places.

A white sand beach with lapping blue waves becomes the place we vacationed with a former lover. The wildflower meadow becomes the field where you broke your ankle playing ultimate Frisbee. The quiet, dusty library full of your favourite literature becomes the place where you crammed for the exam that didn't get you into your first-choice college. I have to imagine that people who really like science fiction have a better chance of finding a happy place than those of us who try to disassociate places in our past from the events or people associated with said places.

Once the cacophonous percussion section began within the ring enveloping my head, I was reminded of the sound of walking into my elementary gymnasium before my first band practice. That noise cascaded like uncontrolled pop-up adverts on a computer screen to my grade six classroom. There I remembered the enormously tall woman who was our teacher helping us to prepare for one state-wide assessment test or another. This was the era when Erhard Seminars Training (EST) was all the rage and our teacher was trying to help us envision ourselves as calm and fully enabled to succeed.

As part of our exercises of preparation, we were asked to meditate, though in conservative western Michigan in the 1970s, 'meditation' was not a word an elementary school teacher wanted students bringing home to Mommy and Daddy. We were told to focus on a calm and peaceful place of our choosing. Less than a year from my St Patrick's Day dressing down by the defender of William the Orange, I created a place of focus in the mystical and far-off land of my imagined ancestors.

Drawing upon books and films I may or may not have actually read or watched, I created an idyllic surrounding. I could retreat there when called upon by the teacher who, we were all sure, could dunk a ball and likely make a half-court shot. My place was more than a location; things happened there and the place made me feel like there were destinations the world had for me outside my little auto-plant city.

My place was against a grey drystone wall that was encrusted with lichen and moss. Blades-long grass stretched through cracks where the unmortared stones met but didn't fit perfectly. Those blades swayed in time with the breeze that came up the hill my wall bisected. That light wind brought the smell of the retreating tide, a smell I could only imagine, having at this age never been to the salt water. The hill receded in short bounces from one slope to the next and down to a shimmering bay.

I would sit with my back against my wall and feel the warmth of the sun on my face and the stored heat of the shale-coloured stones behind me. The waving grass would tickle my face and I would pull out a shoot to nibble on the sweet, tender end of the separated node. As I grew older, using this method and place of escape to prepare for tests, marching band competitions and sporting events throughout my scholastic days, the grass in my hand became a pipe. It wafted a thin, blue line of smoke that smelled of the vanilla Night Lighter tobacco my father packed into his pipes when we would go fishing together.

Sitting in the warm sun and brushed with the cool, salty wind from below, I would be accompanied by my dog. It had always been Boofy in my chosen place, which only made sense. She was my dog if she was anybody's in the family. That she would be with me, watching the sheep bleating on the hillock just below us, made my place complete. It was mine, it was interactive and it was completely fiction, with no worldly attachments to reality and thus to negative experiences.

It was to this far-off wall that I went in my mind's eye to escape my electronic tomb the day of my first MRI – to my wall in Ireland that had served as quiet retreat when I was young but about which I'd forgotten during the ensuing years. Pulled to the side of the small road that led to the farmhouse in the rainbow, I stood and watched the misty cloud that shadowed The Cottage slide down the other side of the valley. Not unlike the cloud that carried the rainbow through The Cottage and up my current side of the glen, it was followed by a rather small shower and brighter air. Beyond the squall I could begin to make out a row of hills. The one row became two and then three. These hills I'd not seen from this angle. Atop the stack of long hillocks I saw a scar of dark, dark grey that ran only a few inches at that distance.

My eyes tried to focus on the mark, but the mist had begun to ascend my current side of the valley and my spectacles were soon speckled with dewy drops. And then the squall was upon me. I know this will sound absurd, but I knew that place; even from that distance and through the mist I felt that the place where the hill was marred by a short blue-black line was a stone wall. Not that I hadn't seen hundreds of miles of drystone walls in my drives and hikes. From the *Ionaid Páirceála* – those lonely blue Ps where Sadie and I sat when hiking or even walking – I could see they were beyond my reach. This wall was different. This wall made me catch my breath. The thought that came to mind made me a little bit dizzy and sick to my stomach.

Perhaps there really could be a place that was exactly as I had imagined it so long ago.

If – and it was as big an if as I'd ever experienced – if this could be even close to my wall, I had to go see it. With the final guest I'll mention arriving at Shannon on the early flight the next morning and the departure preparations I needed to begin, it would have to be a well-scheduled expedition. If the business with my car had swung me around on my anchor, then the capstan of time was beginning to reel in its chain. My wall had been a life raft in desperate times of tests, both academic and medical.

I would find the time to explore the wall on the hill, and if I could not find the time, I would have to make it.

29

The Chemist's Wife

THE CHEMIST'S WIFE was a friend of a friend whom I'd met in the Carolinas. I call her that, not because she was a chemist's wife then, but because she soon would be and is now. We'd been in touch occasionally ever since we met. When, after securing the lease on The Cottage, I put out the call for potential visitors, she answered. I was a little bit surprised that she wanted to come all that way just for the very short period over the American Presidents' Day weekend. Still, the more was always the merrier, and with only Mrs Trinket and me, the house had seemed empty relative to the holidays. She arrived on a Thursday and left the next Monday. The day after that I was to put Mrs Trinket on a train to Dublin. Then I'd spend the last few days tidying up Sadie's affairs before heading back to Seattle ourselves.

It had been implied that I might not need to make up an extra bed for The Chemist's Wife in the months leading up to my departure. I was informed on the return trip from fetching her at the airport, however, that she had met The Chemist at a party a few weeks prior to Christmas and that he was The One. Honestly, I was happy for the girl, and happy for The Chemist too, but I'm not going to lie and say that my winter of celibacy couldn't have done with a bit of a thaw.

She enjoyed the subtle nuances of the country life I'd carved out for myself in The Town, but she mentioned on more than one occasion that she was hoping for the 'Homer Simpson Irish Experience'. Not having seen the particular episode of the long-running animated series, I didn't know the specifics, but I felt pretty comfortable with the assumption that subtlety and nuance weren't part of the script. On the Saturday night of her stay I would treat her to the most caricatured Irish night out I could concoct on short notice featuring a real, not animated, cast of characters.

After a damp afternoon with Sadie playing on the strand, we sat atop a pasture wall on the cliffs at the entrance to The Town's harbour. The sheep in the field behind us were near enough that we could not only smell their scent of damp flannel but could also hear them tearing tufts of grasses from the turf as they munched their way along the piled stones that separated the field from the cliff's face. Sadie sat with us and biblically watched over the flock while The Chemist's Wife and I waved at the parade of returning fishing boats.

Small flocks of grey and white gulls fluttered from just above the mast to behind the transom of each boat as they flew past the harbour mouth. The birds occasionally dived en masse after a scrap of whatever the deckhand might wash or kick from the deck of the boats. We talked mostly about The Chemist as the fishermen prepared their boats to unload at the town's pier so that they might possibly enjoy a night in their own beds before returning to plough again the fertile fields of the North Atlantic. If a first date is a job interview for a relationship, my conversation with The Chemist's Wife felt like an 'informational interview': I wasn't looking to get a 'job' because she wasn't hiring. We'd known each other for a fair bit of time, but I'd never really thought of her as a potential romantic partner until she quipped about not needing an 'extra bed' when we emailed about her stay.

Though there wasn't any real romantic chemistry between us, it felt nice to banter and to flirt a little. I'd had one attempt at a relationship after Beth and I split. That fling was destined for failure because I'd never really gotten over Beth. It sputtered in the months back in Seattle as I prepared for my winter in Kerry. When I'd left, it was on life support.

As The Chemist's Wife sat on our grass-tufted reviewing wall and saluted the returning trawlers and anglers, and we chatted and flirted and simply watched in silence, I wished that it was Beth there with me and Sadie. She had put up with so much as I sank deeper and deeper into self-doubt and felt MS eat away at my former life. Beth had been there for the hardest times after diagnosis – the darkest times. She deserved to be there as things got better. But unlike the boats returning with our dinner, that ship had sailed and it wasn't returning to my port. I had already planned for us to dine on the fruits of the mariners' labour – battered, fried and served with a mound of chips laced with crunchy salt and tart vinegar – for our evening meal. That the boats gave the impression of our main course being so fresh as to virtually flop along from sea to boat to fryer was a herald of our fabled night ahead.

Back at The Cottage, The Chemist's Wife showered and changed for our epic night in town. Meanwhile I stoked the grate with most of the contents of a bag of dug turf we'd purchased from the same filling station where I'd first seen the farmer unloading their cousins nearly a year before. I, of course, told her the story of the farmer and the fields where he dug the sods by hand. I even gave her his name and the names of his children: Sean Patrick, the farmer, and his children, Sean, Patrick, Mary, Malachy and Fiona. If we were going to make this a Homer Simpson experience, why not lay it on thick?

'You can almost smell the heather as his turf burns,' I said when I loaded the sack into the boot of my fifth and final hired car. 'It's the best in the county.'

'Say, Trevis,' she called from the living room while I changed my muddy clothes. 'I see what you were saying about this peat. It really does smell of heather.'

Seriously! Either she was playing the cards I laid down in expert fashion for the fun of the game or Your One had no idea a game was being played at all. The Chemist was either a very lucky man or one who would have to keep a very close eye on his soon-to-be wife. But if I think about it, hadn't I suspended my sense of disbelief for nearly three months? Wasn't I taking everything The Town had to offer at face value? Could it be that I had been living *The Quiet Man* version of The Town just as The Chemist's Wife wanted her *Simpsons* version? Who was I to judge?

Letting go the rails, I dived right into the experience. As I held open the door to the public house I'd chosen for our fish 'n' chips dinner, I opened the door to whatever possibilities the night might have in store.

I waved to the owner whom I'd come to know casually during the many batter-dipped lunches my guests and I shared.

'Hiya, Trevis,' he said from behind the bar. 'Another visitor from America, is it? And a lovely at that,' he continued with a wink that was directed either at me or my friend; I wasn't certain.

My 'date' both beamed and blushed a little bit, and we were waved to a table against the wall. Rule number one of taking someone around 'your' town: only take them to places where people know you. If they seem to like you, that's a bonus too.

Now, you may be thinking, a chef eating fish 'n' chips? Well, let me tell you, good ingredients thoughtfully prepared following the basic laws of cooking methodology – yes, frying is a classic cooking method – is just plain good food. The slabs of fresh fish that arrived at our table, European plaice for me and Atlantic cod for the other side of the table, had been dusted in seasoned flour before being run through batter made with ale from the bar. We were lucky enough to be there on the day the fryer oil was changed. You can tell when oil needs to be changed by the overly dark colour of the food and a 'greasy' look and possibly even flecks of darker coloured stuff that has burned and broken down in the oil. The shatteringly crisp crust was thick enough to give our fillets a yeasty hint of flavour from the beer but not so thick as to hide the flaky white flesh within the golden envelope.

Even though our chips were standard Irish restaurant quality sticks of potato, they were Irish potatoes, which really cannot be beat when it comes to fry-worthy tubers. The side salad that came with the fish wasn't really worth mentioning. Side salads in Ireland seldom, if ever, are worth a mention, let alone the calories, as they are usually dressed pretty thickly. Though neither of us could finish our manhole-cover-sized portions of fish, let alone the alpine peak of chips upon which they were balanced, dessert was in order. To keep with our über-Irish theme of the night, I ordered us a Sticky Toffee Pudding to finish our meal. The dense, date-studded cake is sweet and rich in and of itself. When topped with its namesake toffee sauce made of butter, brown sugar, cream and alcohol, the dish's dark, sweet richness is surrounded by a pool as thin and as pale as my words to describe the dessert. I called for a dram of whiskey to help cut the decadence on our plates only to find that 1) The Chemist's Wife had never had Irish whiskey and 2) she really, REALLY liked it.

I could think of no better place to go after our stereotypic meal of cartoon proportions than the tourist pub where the bartender had explained to me that they weren't offended by Americans trying to get their Irish on. It was perfect for our purposes and even more over the top than I could have hoped for.

Rather than the simple duo of guitar and fiddle or guitar and banjo or guitar and concertina or the ever-popular guitar and guitar, tonight's musical offering was actually quite a show. A local percussionist, I learned, had been giving a workshop on traditional Irish drumming. We must have walked in on some sort of graduation session because there wasn't a thing that had been musically pounded upon for the previous several centuries of Irish music that wasn't being used for drumming.

Several sizes of bodhrán were on knees. A few men played the bones, some being simply wooden versions of spoons that clapped together and some being honest-to-goodness animal bones, by bouncing them in between the heel of the hand and the thigh. Wedged in between the ankles and calves of another man was the old-timey instrument called 'the box,' which was just that – a wooden box that is open on the back and played with different parts of the open hand.

Along with all of these drums, Your Man had assembled several local musicians playing all of the above-mentioned string instruments as well as a mandolin, an accordion and even a small Celtic harp. The corner bench where two players usually sat was augmented with several others into a geometrical mess with most of the musicians facing one another rather than the rest of the room. The place was once again mostly filled with locals rather than tourists, owing to the time of year, I suppose. The numbers rivalled the night of Women's Christmas, though the gender mix was closer to even this time.

The music in The Town was always very good. On this night the good became great and you could feel that something quite special was happening. Players would sit out songs they did not know and watch others playing their parts to learn. Toe-tapping became outright stomping during some songs, and soon the dancing began.

Couples began to spin and sets formed. Here and there farmers and shopkeepers, bachelor labourers and married professionals, throngs of them, began to step-dance the hard-shoe dances they learned in school. The low-slung ceiling of the rooms kept the dancers from jumping too high, but otherwise we're talking full-on Riverdance stuff here.

We both switched over to sparkling water by the bottleful as the heat and personal humidity of the pub climbed to Amazonian reaches. Others in the room, particularly one table of Germans camped on a bench between the fireplace and the band, quelled the increasing swelter by increasing the pace of their intake as well, only it wasn't water in their pint glasses.

One of their party, a very tall, very thin man with sparse wisps of blond hair and limbs that seemed to dangle from the top and bottom of his torso, unfolded himself from the table. It was either his round to buy or time for a nature call to make room for his next. The scarecrow of a man had to duck as he crossed under the open archway leading from the musicians' room to the next and then on along the corridor to the toilets. I say 'scarecrow', but the way his extremities moved about and his head bobbled above his shoulders when he passed, it was as if his joints had been lubricated by the tin woodsman's oilcan. As the drinking-up hour was fast approaching, I asked The Chemist's Wife if she'd like another drink. We had consumed nothing but water for a couple of hours and perspired enough, so I saw no harm in joining her in a glass of her newly discovered spirit.

'No, not yet. I don't think so,' was her answer, so I went to replace our empty bottles of water with two more of the same. As I negotiated the substantial but manageable crowd from the bar to our perch in front of the archway where Lubricated Man had passed us a few minutes before, I found myself on an intercept track with his returning self. We made eye contact like two drivers approaching an unregulated intersection and motioned each other the right of way. Our stopping and starting as we followed each other's offering was accented by the waggle of his arms and legs with each false step.

At some point we both – but I think he first – realised that we were stepping, and thus his arms swinging, in close proximity to the rhythm of the music. He looked at his feet and hands as if they were new to him or possibly even someone else's as they moved to the omnipresent beat. It was with a certain amount of wonder, as if he had never seen nor felt his body moving to music before, that he looked at me and smiled the smile of intoxicated joy.

And then he was off.

Ducking his head under the arch and trying as best he could to mimic the stiff arms of traditional Irish step dancing, he entered into the musicians' room like a marionette on a springboard. For a few moments, as he paid what attention he had to the task at hand, he wasn't all that bad. He was on, or at least very near, the beat, and while his moves were as exaggerated as his body, they made some musical sense. Once he realised that he had the attention of the room, his attention shifted to all of us and our reactions rather than the all-important music.

He danced in a kind of syncopation to the music that reminded me of the two loudspeakers at opposite ends of the Main Street hill at Christmas. He was close but not close enough. The harder he tried to catch up or slow down to the beat, the very distance his thought had to travel from his head to his feet seemed to get in the way. But he did not stop. He stomped and stumbled, bounced and bobbed. I felt bad when for a short few steps he caught up to the rhythm, only to lose it more completely than before.

Though he had the steady clapping of the whole room urging him on in unison, it was something of a mercy when the set ended and the lights of the bar popped on to signal that the drinking-up hour had been reached. The room erupted in applause, for the dancer at first, but then in real appreciation of the band and their extraordinary efforts. Your Man continued to take bows until some of his tablemates retrieved him from his one-man dance floor.

'You wanted Homer Simpson's Ireland,' I said as I reached for our coats. 'I think you got your wish.'

'Where to next?' she asked after laughing the entire time it took to dress for the cold.

'That's it,' I said. 'It's eleven. The pubs close at eleven here, even on the weekend.'

Even though she knew – and she knew that I knew – that the purring that came next was harmless and playful, a little part of me worried for The Chemist if we did go for one more. You just don't take advantage of another man's woman when he's far away. Putting that concern aside, I quickly ushered her out the door and up road to the pub of the 'broken clock' for one final round. If she continued to purr, I wouldn't mind. I hadn't had any purring in a long time.

Not a few of us traversed from the tourist pub to The Clock, but we were quick enough to the door that we found seats, while most of the others had to stand. I ordered Herself a dram and a pint for me. I noticed that a few of the patrons at the bar had more than one and in some cases more than two glasses two-thirds full of porter sitting in front of them. I asked the publican what all the partial construction was about.

'We stop selling drinks at eleven,' He informed me. 'No guard in the Free Irish Nation would stop me from finishing off a man's pint for him if it wasn't quite done at the appointed hour now, would he?'

The skirting of the law did not end with the perpetual running behind of the official timepiece, it would appear. As the hour approached, I felt the need to get in on the fun and ordered myself a couple of beers and an extra for Herself as well. I had no intention of finishing them both off because I was driving. With that thought, I remembered the sober taxi man's card in my wallet, so the idea wasn't a total non-starter. In the end, I only had the one and The Chemist's Wife opted for another whiskey at last call.

As we sat on our stools, which we had draped with our coats, we laughed at the spectacle that played itself out for us that evening.

'In all my time here, and even in trips before this one,' I honestly admitted, 'I have never even heard of a night like this, let alone been a part of one.'

Sure, there was the night in Dublin with my parents a couple of years prior. My father sheepishly knocked on my door the next morning, fully expecting both of the English women from the pub where we were all having a good time the night before to be in my room.

'They're not here, Da,' I said in answer to him peeking around my shoulders through the open door. 'Not any more …'

To this day my father tells the story as if the ladies had scurried from my room just moments before his arrival. Some things we just let our fathers think.

But the truth of the matter is that the night I took The Chemist's Wife out for a made-up, over-the-top night in The Town turned out to be the most real of over-the-top extravaganzas. And then we were treated to what Americans think of as a quintessential Irish curtain call.

Among a group of young and rather attractive tourist women stood a man who could have stepped straight out of central casting. Tufts of carrot-ginger hair sprouted from beneath his cap that closely – but not closely enough

– matched the tweed of his jacket. His face and eyes were equally round, though his chin showed a shadow of his former, chiselled self. His cheeks matched his nose with a light shade of cardinal.

He cleared his throat once for purpose and then one more time, louder, for effect and hummed a beautiful low C. Then he cleared his throat again.

The tenor then snuck up on the note with a long, soft but rising, 'OooooooooOOOh,' which he followed in the most beautiful timbre, 'Danny Booooooooooy' and so on with the song.

You don't hear 'Danny Boy' sung much in Ireland. It's not like you hear people in Virginia popping off 'Shenandoah' in bars, or 'My Old Kentucky Home' at a Lexington barbecue joint. But there it was, being sung to the now-hushed crowd, who had all stopped what they were doing to listen.

Not everyone in the bar approved of Your Man's choice of song. A local woman near us said rather loudly in the gap that happens as soon as a song is finished but before the applause deafens the room, 'AH, fer FECK'S SAKE, it's not like it's feckin' really an Irish feckin' song!' followed by an exasperated and prolonged, 'Fheeeeeeeeck!'

This drew a few quick laughs, but was lost to clapping and shouts of 'Well done!' for our troubadour.

Though it was evident by the glasses some of our fellow patrons had on deck and in the hole that the evening could go on for quite a while longer, we decided to call it a night and call ourselves that taxi. Before leaving, though, I slid the two partially built pint glasses to the lad next to me and wished him a good night and the same to the tender of the taps. We tried to make our way over to the tenor, but his gathering of young women had grown and there was no need to interfere with the well-won adoration.

We stepped out of the pub and into the night and slipped out of what felt like a drunken dream and into the sober cab.

30

A Promise (To Herself and Myself)

I'VE HEARD IT SAID THAT a *smart* man learns from his mistakes but a wise one learns from the mistakes of others. While it is indeed my aspiration to one day attain such wisdom, for the purposes of this day, 'smart' was enough.

After returning his future wife to The Chemist and depositing Mrs Trinket and her MS on a train bound for Dublin, I set my attention to learning the lesson of making my way to the rainbow house. In the snippets of time in between returning borrowed puppy stuff to Sadie's breeder, getting all of her EU Pet Passport and immunisation documents in order, settling utility bills with The Princess, sorting and packing, I searched the *Sraith Eolais* for roads that might lead me to – or at least near – my wall. Neither road nor trail was marked, and the topography seemed rather steep. Whenever my shrinking schedule allowed, I would drive along one route or another to see how close I might come.

The map had been so accurate and helpful to me over the prior three months that I was surprised to find an unmarked path beyond one of the roads that the map showed winding to an end. I guess it was really more than a path but far less than a 'road'. The way this dodgy thoroughfare cut across the hillside deterred me from turning the rental onto it, but at least I could see that the hiking might be made easier by some margin. Destination known, road chosen and access confirmed, I would spend my next and penultimate day in The Town seeking out a place of childhood fantasy.

Heartily breakfasted and loaded down with bottled water and snacks, Sadie and I set off for the end of the marked road and the beginning of an unknown path. We parked the rental just before the unmarked bit and began to cross the field. Within twenty yards or so the path, which was marked with what looked like truck tyre tracks, bent behind a rise and I could no longer see the car. It was at that point that it became obvious why the way had been forged.

Around that corner the hills and fields fed themselves into a flat and open ancient bog. Wet with the midwinter rains, there was no one digging the land and only a few sods of turf strewn around the trenches. The path itself was much more drivable at this point and I could see that it continued for about a quarter of a mile beyond where we stood. I also saw, beyond the brown-black scar in the earth where men had recently dug fuel, that my wall was much closer to the end of that road than I had expected it to be. It was also fitted atop a much steeper hill than I had imagined … or hoped for.

As early as breakfast, I could already feel the day's energy balance draining away from me. Rather than spend it on a half-mile return walk, I retreated to the car and attempted to make it past the first rough part to where the way was flat. A few uncomfortable bumps and maybe one major bottoming-out – but, eh, it's a rental! – and we were riding along the tractor path as though we belonged there. I was glad for the decision, as my estimation of distance fell far short. We drove closer to a mile than to a half – for the bends and turns of the road – to the place where the diggers had made a turnaround for their vehicles.

Invisible from the distance of our prior posting was a sheep path that ran past, but very near to, the makeshift car park. Once again Sadie and I embarked, with our pack and two sturdy walking sticks, on our journey.

Expending far less energy and time than I had budgeted, we reached the crest of the hill adjacent to our destination. I looked across the valleys and glens toward the west and saw the rainbow house and the spot on their road where I had first spied the ruin. It was, indeed, more than a wall; it looked like the remains of a shepherd's shelter or maybe the fallen pen where sheep had once been held for shearing. Whatever it was, it was close, and my view of the surrounding hills and valleys was like nothing I'd seen in the three months of my stay.

I could see for quite a distance in every direction from where we stood, and saw no apparent reason for Herself to stay on her lead. I unclipped the hook from her collar and we began to walk. She sensed the freedom and began to run circles around me. With her tail tucked under her bum and that bum subsequently tucked low under her legs, Sadie increased the size of her orbits and made them more and more elliptical. She settled on a path that brought her within ten feet of my beam on each side but cut closer to my stern as she passed. Those distances remained constant as the forward end of her loop took her thirty or more yards away from me.

She ran with a passion and enthusiasm I would have matched in the days I could still run. I was beginning to have trouble just keeping my current pace walking our path without stumbling over the smallest rock or tuft of heather. The racing of Sadie's legs and her heart was matched, however, by the happiness that rose in me as I watched. She would slow as she neared me at each lap and then accelerate as she shot around me from behind. With a little work and a trained hand, Sadie would no doubt have made a fine herding dog – one of the many laudable traits for which Wheatens are known.

By the time we came up the side of the next bump on the hill where the stones lay – some stacked, some askew – Sadie had stopped herding me and was now sitting at the far apex of her turn to await my increasingly staggered arrival. She would then again tear around me and park herself ten or so yards ahead and do it all over again. Finally she disappeared off the hill just beyond my sight. Like a worried father, I stopped and called for her to return. The furry face that peeked at me from over my visible horizon was as happy a puppy face as you've ever seen. She bounded down and jumped at me from a spot about shoulder height from above.

Dropping my sticks, I caught her wriggling self in my arms and fell into the soft, prickly heather. I was rewarded with a shower of kisses from my happy and panting little girl. I set her down next to me, where she rolled over on her back to be scratched. I don't know if I'd felt happier at any point in my life. She popped up to offer more sloppy affection as I attempted to get up on my feet. Back down I went, and I could feel how much she had grown since the first time she'd jumped onto my chest in the gutter in front of B&B#2 on our pyjamaed trek her first morning in The Town. My puppy was nearly six months old already and I wondered where the time had gone. 'I promise you,' I vowed into her big, brown eyes set into her white mask and not yet covered by an adult fall, 'I will bring you back here. This is your home, Sadie. It's our home and I will bring you back.'

The promise was as much to myself as it was to Sadie, but it was no less an oath to my wonderful companion's spirit.

The wall – or whatever it was, but we'll go with 'wall' – was not the place I had created in my mind nearly thirty years before; little of our childhood fantasy ever is. It was at the same time less than and greater than the wall of my happy place. That's all we can really strive for in life, isn't it? We take that for which we hope, mix it with experiences both good and bad and see if any bits of reality can stick to our fantasy.

The view from the brow of the hillock where the stones lay mostly stacked was indeed a bounding one, down from this hill to the next and several in succession to the sea. The stones were dark and dead. They were more of the landscape than those in my head that had, over the imagined centuries, become part of their surrounds, not simply placed upon them. Pellets of sheep droppings made it difficult to find a place to sit, but Sadie and I found a spot that was relatively clear and I resigned myself to doing another load of laundry that last evening.

The real wall was not warmed with sun. It was cold, and I could feel the warmth of my body migrating through my jumper and coat into the gelid rock.

Sadie bounced around the hillside as I dug into my pocket for the pipe I'd filled and stuffed away for this moment. The gentle breeze was really a wind that came up from the salty water. It was brisk and cold and it was the smell of rain, rather than receding tide, that it carried. I made several attempts to light wooden matches for my briar, but after many failures I just stuffed the pipe back into my pocket along with the spent sticks.

No blades of green grass danced or brushed against me. Scraggy tufts of tundra plants poked through rocks, small clumps of heather anchored themselves against the Atlantic winds, and the burnt remnants of the invasive gorse bushes – often set ablaze by farmers to clear an area for grazing – lay on a short, sheep-clipped carpet of the barest grass.

This was a much harder place than I had imagined it being. As with looking back on life in general, most things are harder than we think they will be when we are young. I surely never considered the prospect of living the rest of my days fighting my own immune system. I wouldn't have envisioned divorce or the relationship difficulties that continued. But at the same time, the reality of my wall offered a comforting beauty to balance the harshness of reality.

Sadie came around the wall licking her chops, for she had probably found a scattering of sheep shite fresh enough for her liking, and lay at my feet with her chin across my legs. I could not feel her on my numb left leg, but the deep sigh of contentment she let out travelled up my right side and straight to my heart.

Getting what we need out of life has as much to do with what we take from it as what we are given. Living life with a chronic illness is all about taking back. I do not believe that my illness can be cured with the butterfly farts and unicorn piss of the 'attitude is everything' believers. I did not cause my disease by my actions and I cannot cure it by them either. I can, however, try to find the beauty in my new life.

Multiple sclerosis did not steal my future. MS robbed me of the future I had intended to have. The responsibility for what happens next – experiences, loves, the impact on others around me – those are things that are still in my control. Like 'my' wall, which is nothing like I had created yet everything I actually needed, the task a winter in Ireland had set for me was in finding the beauty in the things for which I had not planned and the importance in having a plan in the first place.

I came to realise the truth of the statement I made to you in the introduction: 'Hope without a plan is just a dream.'

My childhood dream had been to visit one day a land my ancestors had left longer ago than the history I studied in Mrs Magee's class. That dream had become a hope that I might be able to live that dream before multiple sclerosis robbed me of the ability to travel and enjoy the people and places of this magical island. Only with the help of doctors, nurses, researchers, friends and family, and the love of the dear one who had first given me a taste of this 'home', had I been able to create a plan to make them all come true.

My disease will progress. As my doctor once said to me, 'Aggressive MS doesn't become benign MS, Trevis.' I can accept that as a pragmatic person. I, too, will progress, thanks to the experiences I gained during my winter in Kerry. Aggressively, I determined, would also be the way I'd fight to retain what MS has not taken and to regain what might be taken back. I was given a gift of staying in The Cottage, a gift made more special for the people who came to experience The Town with me. And my dream was made real by the wonderful, genuine, quirky people who welcomed me into their town, if only for a short time. It was my duty then, as much to myself as to them, to live fully the life they had helped me realise.

The next day would have Sadie and me chasing the sun all the way to America's west coast, as I once had chased it from Kiev to San Francisco in search of a new job and a fresh start after Sheri and I separated. The Town hadn't ended my search, not for this wall, nor had it quelled my desire to live amongst its residents. The time had been too short. That I was thinking of eighty-nine days as 'short', in retrospect, was evidence that the seeds of my desire weren't simply scattered there, in the hills and valleys of west Kerry. They had been planted in rich soil, tended by caring friends, new and old, and they had been watered … Oh, aye; they had been very well watered.

I am not finished trying to live my life the best I am able, and Sadie and I are not finished with Ireland … and I've made a promise.

PART VII

The Journey Ends: Sweet Recipes

31

Pudding (Dessert) Recipe

I WOULD HAVE RATHER STAYED in The Town, but like a great meal, my time there had come to an end. While my preference is always for another helping of savoury stew rather than pudding, some people require a sweet to end their great meal. A snapshot I took of Sadie at the top of that hill while I rested against the wall serves as my long, sweet dessert of that winter. One of her ears was caught by the breeze and flipped straight up while the other remained folded down. It's almost as if she's waving goodbye to Kerry in that shot.

I offer one last recipe as a way to end our story. I'd searched for this formula for a long time. A pudding very much like it was shared with Beth on my first trip to Ireland as well as ordered with The Chemist's Wife on this trip. It is intensely rich and sweet, but a slight bitterness in the toffee sauce blunts the sharpest edge of the sugar sword.

Bake the cakes in buttered and lightly floured ramekins (6 oz/70 g size) in a roasting pan that you've lined with a clean tea towel, for best results.

I hope you enjoy it.

—Sticky Toffee Pudding—

Serves 8

For the cakes

80g/3 oz/²/₃ cup pitted dates, chopped roughly

180ml/6 fl oz/¾ cup warm water

¼+ teaspoon baking soda (a well-rounded ¼ teaspoon will work)

80g/3 oz/²/₃ cup pitted dates, sliced about 0.5 cm/¼ inch thick

140g/5 oz/¾ cup dark brown sugar (well packed)

2 large eggs

1¾ teaspoons vanilla

½ teaspoon table salt

60g/2 oz/4 tablespoons unsalted butter, melted

160g/5½ oz/1¼ cup plain flour, sifted

½ teaspoon baking powder

For the toffee sauce

110g/4 oz/1 stick unsalted butter

210g/7½ oz/1 cup dark brown sugar

2 tablespoons Irish whiskey

140g/5 oz/²/₃ cup cream

1 teaspoon lemon zest, finely grated

Method

For the cakes

Preheat oven to 180°C/350°F/Gas 4.

Mix the chopped dates with warm water and baking soda. Soak, stirring now and again, for 5 minutes.

Drain (reserving the liquid) and place softened dates into a teacup.

Place sliced dates in a large bowl with about half the brown sugar and mash with the back of a fork until mostly incorporated.

Add remaining sugar, eggs, vanilla, and reserved soaking liquid to date-sugar mixture and stir until well mixed.

Stir melted butter into mixture.

Fold in softened dates and salt.

Sift flour and baking powder together into a second bowl.

Mix dry ingredients into the wet mixture.

Set the kettle on to boil.

Divide batter between 8 prepared ramekins (they'll be about half full).

Place cakes on top of a clean tea towel in a large roasting pan with sides of at least 2 inches but no more than 4 inches.

Pour boiling water from kettle into the roasting pans – taking care not to get water in the cakes – to reach the level of the cakes inside their ramekins.

Cover pan with a tight fitting lid or wrap tightly with aluminium foil.

Bake until they look like pancakes ready to flip (bubbles have burst leaving small holes); 30–50 minutes depending on the day.

Remove to a clean, dry tea towel on the counter to cool.

For the toffee sauce

Melt butter in a heavy-bottomed saucepan over low heat.

Increase heat to medium and stir in brown sugar.

Cook and continue to stir until smooth, dissolved, and beginning to darken.

Take off heat and stir in whiskey (take particular care if you are near an open flame, as the booze can ignite).

Return to low heat and whisk in cream in a slow, steady stream.

Stir until sauce just begins to froth, but not until it boils, for it will easily break (about 3 minutes).

Keep warm.

To Serve

Run a thin blade around the cake and invert onto a dessert plate.

Top with a few tablespoons of sauce.

🍂 🍂 🍂

Also, as promised, here is the recipe for Irish whiskey and blood orange marmalade. You don't have to use top-shelf whiskey for this, but the subtle flavour of whiskey is important to the final product, so don't chose the rotgut stuff either. If you decide to dilute the whiskey with water as is offered as an option, use at least half whiskey for that same reason.

As well as all of the other 'regular' uses for marmalade – topping for toast and scones, etc. – I really love this spread warmed with an equal amount of butter into a rich syrup to top the self-raising pancakes in the baking chapter – particularly if I've added bacon to the pancake batter!

—Irish Whiskey Marmalade —

Makes 10–12 jars

900g/2 lb blood oranges

2 lemons

3 bottles Irish whiskey plus 1 litre of water (COOL to COLD)

3.6kg/8 lb sugar

1 pinch sea salt

Method

Day 1

Wipe fruit clean, cut in half (pole to pole) and again (from pole to pole) to make long quarters.

Remove pips and reserve in a teacup or ramekin. Cover pips with water and store at room temperature.

Slice fruit (oranges and lemons) across the grain to make wedge slices (very thin to ¼ inch). The thickness of your slices will determine the texture of the finished marmalade.

Place fruit in a large, non-reactive pot (i.e. steel, but not aluminium or iron. The acids will react badly to them). and pour in whiskey. Cover for at least 24 hrs.

Day 2

Place pips in a piece of muslin, cheesecloth or the like and pour water into fruit.

Tie cloth and submerge the pip sachet in fruit and whiskey.

Bring to a hard boil, then turn off immediately and cover.

Leave at room temperature for 24–36 hours.

Day 3

Uncover and bring to a boil.

Remove from heat and stir in sugar until mostly dissolved.

Bring back to a boil.

Cover, remove from heat and leave at room temp for 24 hours.

Day 4

Uncover, remove cloth holding pips and bring to a boil until marmalade gels when tested on a cold plate/saucer (at least 45 minutes).

Seal the jars with proper lids and process in boiling water for 10 minutes. Allow to cool and then store.

Goodbye to Kerry.

Epilogue

EVERY HALLOWEEN WE paid special reverence to a house on the next block from my childhood home. There the mother of Roger B. Chaffee – one of the three astronauts who perished in the launch-pad fire that consumed the Apollo 1 spacecraft – would hand out candy while a larger-than-life oil portrait of her son in his spacesuit smiled down at us.

Mine was a generation of American boys who came up drinking Tang and dreaming of walking on the moon or orbiting Earth in Skylab. While I never slipped the bounds of Earth's gravity, my re-entry to my former world was no less dramatic to me. Departing my antiquated Cottage on the side of a road once nothing more than – and still quite akin to – a sheep's path, I strapped in and chased the sun westward to Seattle.

A speedy airline change in Boston gave Sadie her first chance to smell America. She peed on it.

We'd taken off from the Ireland of pony traps, turf fires and cups of tea with neighbours. We landed in Seattle, America, three days before the Seahawks' first ever Super Bowl game. Not only did I not know what time it was or even day of the week, I had the feeling I'd left one world and arrived in another world decades later.

The thieves who took my Jetta on a burglary spree had had quite a time with it, judging from the contents of the boot listed in the police report. Though the shop had a month to repair the damage, it still took a week before that was sorted. The car was never the same, nor was its driver.

The Swiss who sublet my flat while I was away became dear friends and have remained close even after they moved back to their homeland.

While boisterous retellings of individual and collective antics can be heard from all of our guests, there is a hushed reverence when any of us speak together of our time there. I was not the only short-term resident of the Mountain Road Cottage who was changed by The Town. I can only hope that we had a little positive effect on its residents as well. I'm sure that they were at least amused.

Though she missed the sheep, Sadie settled into our Ballard neighbourhood without a thought. Forever the puppy, she is always at my side, always happy to see me if I've been away and always ready for our next adventure. Her needs make getting out of the house an important part of my days. On the 'bad days' – the times when MS keeps me out of the larger world – she makes the world inside the house bright and happy.

Like any good accomplice, Sadie would never betray the stories I have omitted from this telling. She would not recount the tears I have shed or admit to her hand in winning her new mother's heart. In return for her loyalty, for her companionship, for her spirit, and because I am a man of my word, I have kept my promise to her. I have brought her home to west Kerry, and she now has a Wheaten sister called Newkdara Sister Mary Margaret. 'Maggie.'

Acknowledgments

FORTUNATE IS THE MAN given a page to thank people for their assistance in producing a work such as this. The list is long, but I would be crushed by the very mass of a list containing those who will remain unnamed.

The combined team of Marilyn Allen, Jennifer McCord and Sheryl Stebbins has helped me take this work from concept to publisher-ready with all the scheduled and unanticipated stops along the way. Thank you, Dear Ladies of this business beyond the words.

At my lowest point – the year before this story began – Erin Poznanski, Patty Shepherd-Barnes and so many others from the National MS Society helped me to find a place in the world again and the opportunity to give back. This story wouldn't have happened without them.

My health team includes Dr James Bowen, MD, Bobbie Severson, ARNP, and Michelle Toshima PhD. Body, mind and spirit have been attended to by these committed multiple sclerosis professionals, and for this I am forever grateful.

Rose Pike, Carolynn Delaney, Natalie Cagle and Katie Sullivan Guenther – originally with Health Talk and then Everyday Health – first got me to tell my story and have helped to create the Life with MS Community.

To that, the thousands of people living with multiple sclerosis who made the Life with MS Community a worldwide 'thing' have been a daily inspiration to my writing. Had you not continued to find our pages, read, share, comment and become that 'community,' this work would never have happened.

To Bethany Spinler, who first brought me to Ireland, to the friends and family who visited The Cottage and left a bit of their story for me to tell, and to the residents of 'The Town,' who welcomed, became my friends and continue to make me feel at home, I am forever grateful.

Helen Hubbock brought Sadie into my life, continues to be a dear friend and has since 'mothered' our new puppy, Maggie, who as with most children, I suppose, is wonderfully nothing like her sister at all.

Dearest of friends, Holly Hill 'lent' me time in Terry and Connie Shipp's vacation home when quiet space was required. Tracey Higdon and Jodi Chmielewski, on the other hand, offered boisterous accommodation when no other would have done.

The recipes herein were tested by dear friends Heather L. Jones and Jason Anderson. These two chefs made sure that I am not the only person who can make the recipes work. The food is better for their notes.

Finally, it takes a special woman to fall in love with a guy like me. Caryn did just that at the time in my life when I was ready to love again. She has been supportive in a way that only writers can understand, only the most fortunate ever experience and of which only saints are worthy. Thank you, Petal.